STORIES OF

Miraculous
TRANSFORMATION

FROM THOSE WHO BROKE THROUGH THE IMPOSSIBLE

COMPILED BY TRUNNIS GOGGINS II

FOREWORD

It is difficult not to sense that something in the world feels unsettled. War stretches across borders. Abuse continues to surface in homes and institutions. Grief lingers in communities in ways that are hard to name. Trauma is more visible than it once was, yet no less heavy. It accumulates quietly, then all at once.

At times, it feels as though the ground beneath us is shifting.

Yet fracture is not foreign to the earth. Volcanoes rupture. Tectonic plates press and release. Forests burn and regenerate. Beneath every visible eruption lies a long season of invisible pressure. The natural world does not label these moments as failure. It absorbs them into its rhythm. We, however, often experience disruption as something that has gone wrong rather than something that is unfolding.

When pressure rises in our own lives, instinct takes over. We brace. We protect. We withdraw. Protection is human. It keeps us safe in the immediate moment. What we can change is what we tell ourselves afterwards. We cannot always stop the rupture, but we can change the story that says, *"This is how it will always be."*

This is where our understanding of miracles narrows.

We reserve the word for the spectacular: survival against odds, sudden reversals, outcomes that defy logic. We wait for something external to intervene. We imagine miracles as events that arrive fully formed.

But what if a miracle is not only what happens to us, nor a single heroic act?

What if it is the interpretation we choose after the ground has shifted, and the direction we move because of it?

A seismic event can break a person, but it can also reveal them. The difference is rarely in the event itself, but in the response that follows. In the questions asked. In the decision to harden or to open. To repeat or to interrupt. To carry forward harm or to transform it into something that does not wound the next generation.

Miracles are not interruptions of reality; they are redirections within it. They are the quiet moments when someone refuses to let pain dictate identity. The decision to seek help rather than collapse into silence. The choice to forgive without denying what happened. The courage to speak when secrecy once felt safer. The discipline to rebuild trust where betrayal once stood. The resolve to ensure that what hurt you will not become what shapes others.

These movements rarely look dramatic and can be cumulative. They unfold privately and are decisions repeated under pressure until a new foundation forms. A conversation initiated. A boundary set. A pattern noticed and dismantled. A small act of care offered without applause. A cycle ended without announcement.

Left unexamined, pain becomes pattern. Pattern becomes culture. Culture becomes legacy. Yet courage works the same way. A single reframed story can shift a family. An interrupted habit can alter a lineage. A single act of compassion can soften a hardened environment. Over time, these choices create new ground for others to stand on.

The voices in this book did not escape pressure. Each encountered their own version of rupture, loss, betrayal, illness, injustice, or fear. What unites them is not the scale of what occurred, but their refusal to let that moment define its meaning or their future.

They could not always control the event. None of us can. What they could shape was their interpretation, their response, and the direction that followed. That is where transformation took root.

These stories do not present perfection. They reveal process and show how a single decision, made when everything feels unstable, can become the hinge on which an entire future turns. They remind us that transformation is less about spectacle and more about stewardship, of our energy, our anger, our grief, our fear, and our love.

Anger can divide or protect. Fear can isolate or sharpen awareness. Grief can close a heart or deepen it. The force itself is not the miracle but what we allow it to become.

As you read, there is no demand that you experience something dramatic. There is only an invitation to notice. Where have you allowed an event to define you? Where are you bracing when you could be rebuilding? Where are you waiting for rescue when you are already standing at the threshold of response?

Transformation rarely announces itself. It often begins with a small shift, a different question, a quieter reaction, a refusal to continue what once felt automatic.

Miracles are not reserved for extraordinary people. They are forged in ordinary moments by those who decide that what happened will inform them but not imprison them.

This book exists because the authors chose movement over stagnation and meaning over silence. They did not erase what occurred. They reshaped what would flow forward.

May their stories remind you that the ground can shift without you collapsing with it. That interpretation carries power. That action compounds. And that sometimes the most profound miracle is not the event itself, but the person you become in response to it.

With fire and a steady belief in you and your story of miraculous transformation,

Twee Shaw

Certified ProCoach, Life Coach, and Master NLP Practitioner and trauma-informed coach

https://zeniful.com.au/

TABLE OF CONTENTS

TRANSFORMATION

A CATALYST FOR PURPOSE

If a reader has spent time with my books, The 4Ps of You and Lessons From My Father, they will already know that there was a period in my life that felt overwhelmingly dark. It was a time when direction seemed absent, and purpose felt distant. In The 4Ps of You, I briefly reference that chapter of my life, offering only a glimpse into the internal struggles that shaped my thinking. In Lessons From My Father, I explore those experiences in greater detail. Yet even in those reflections, it can be difficult to fully explain what that period felt like from the inside.

On the surface, my life appeared stable. I was fulfilling my responsibilities and doing everything that was expected of me. I was working, providing for my family, and meeting the practical demands of adulthood. Yet beneath that outward stability, there existed a quiet emptiness. It was the unsettling realization that although I was moving through life, I did not feel deeply connected to a clear sense of purpose.

Strangely, this season lasted longer than it should have. Looking back now, I often wonder why it took so long for me to break free from that state of uncertainty. There was nothing catastrophic happening in my life that forced immediate change. Instead, it was more like drifting in calm waters without a compass. Days passed, responsibilities were met, but the deeper question of purpose remained unanswered.

The turning point arrived in an unexpected way through a book.

I came across a biography written by historian Jean Edward Smith titled Grant. The book is a comprehensive study of the life of Ulysses S. Grant, one of the most important military leaders in American history and later the eighteenth President of the United States. At first, I approached the book simply as an interesting historical narrative. I had always enjoyed reading about history, and the life of Grant seemed worthy of exploration.

What I did not anticipate was how deeply the story would affect me.

Smith's biography does not present Grant as a flawless hero. Instead, it reveals the full complexity of the man. The narrative walks through moments of success, but also through periods of hardship, doubt, and personal struggle. The more I read, the more I realized that Grant's life story was not simply about military triumph. It was about resilience and transformation.

One particular episode in the book captured my attention in a way that I could not ignore.

In June of 1854, Ulysses S. Grant was likely forced to resign from the United States Army due to issues related to alcohol. For a professional soldier whose identity had been shaped by military service, this was a devastating moment. Grant returned home not as a celebrated officer but as a man who carried the weight of personal disgrace. His career had collapsed, and his financial situation was bleak.

When he arrived home, he was essentially penniless.

The years that followed were not kind to him. Grant attempted several different ventures in an effort to support his family. He tried farming. He worked in various positions that provided only modest income. Many of those efforts failed to bring the stability he desperately needed. During this period, Grant experienced the quiet humiliation of a man who once held promise but now struggled to regain his footing.

It is easy to imagine how such circumstances could have permanently defined him.

Yet history unfolded differently.

Less than ten years after returning home in disgrace, the United States found itself in the midst of the Civil War. When the conflict began, Grant sought to return to military service. The path back into the army was not smooth. His earlier resignation had created doubts among those who evaluated him. Some questioned his character. Others questioned his ability to lead.

Grant himself was not immune to those doubts. Internal uncertainty accompanied him as he attempted to rebuild his reputation. Humility became a necessary companion during this process. He had to prove himself again, step by step, without the benefit of the prestige he once held.

Despite the skepticism surrounding him, Grant began demonstrating a unique approach to leadership. His thinking was unconventional compared to many of his contemporaries. While others hesitated or adhered rigidly to traditional tactics, Grant often displayed a willingness to take calculated risks. He believed in persistent pressure and decisive action.

Gradually, his leadership began producing results.

Battle after battle demonstrated that his instincts for strategy and persistence were remarkably effective. The same man who had once returned home penniless and disgraced was now commanding armies with clarity and determination. His ability to remain steady under pressure set him apart from many other commanders.

Eventually, Grant rose to hold the highest rank of any military officer in the history of the United States Army up to that point. As General-in-Chief of the Union forces, he played a decisive role in preserving the Union during the Civil War. His leadership and determination helped shape the outcome of the conflict and altered the course of American history.

What struck me most as I read Smith's biography was not simply the scale of Grant's achievements. It was the transformation that occurred between his lowest moment and his greatest success.

Grant's story reminded me that failure does not have the final word in a person's life. Transformation rarely occurs through a single dramatic moment. Instead, it unfolds through perseverance, humility, and the willingness to continue moving forward despite doubt.

The journey from disgraced officer to national hero did not come easily for Grant. It required him to endure external skepticism from superiors who questioned his decisions. It required him to wrestle with his own internal doubts. It required him to accept the reality of past mistakes while still believing that his future could be different.

Yet through that process, he changed.

Reading that story became a catalyst for change in my own life. Grant's transformation challenged me to reconsider how I viewed my own circumstances. If a man who had once returned home in disgrace could rise again through perseverance and purpose, then perhaps the quiet lack of direction I felt in my own life was not permanent.

Perhaps it was simply the beginning of a new chapter.

Grant's life reminded me that purpose is not always something we are handed easily. Sometimes it is discovered through reflection and persistence. Sometimes it appears only after we decide to move forward, even when the path ahead feels uncertain.

In many ways, that realization became the starting point of my own transformation.

The Power of Transformation

The story of Ulysses S. Grant did more than simply interest me as a reader. It became a catalyst for change in my own life. His journey from disgrace to leadership intersected with a series of events unfolding in my personal world at the same time. Together, those influences created the beginning of a transformation that would ultimately benefit not only my own life but also the generations that would follow me. What began as a quiet internal shift slowly grew into a new way of thinking about purpose, responsibility, and the kind of legacy a person leaves behind.

I have always been drawn to stories of redemption. There is something deeply human about witnessing someone rise from hardship and reshape the direction of their life. Redemption stories remind us that the worst moment in a person's life does not have to define the rest of it. They demonstrate that people are capable of growth, renewal, and meaningful change. That belief has shaped much of the work I do today. Even my podcast is built around this idea. Episode after episode features individuals who have transformed themselves personally, professionally, spiritually, or emotionally. Each guest brings a story that reflects the resilience of the human spirit.

One of my favorite movies captures that idea of redemption perfectly. The Shawshank Redemption has always stood out to me as one of the most powerful films ever created. The story follows a man who endures years of unjust imprisonment yet refuses to allow those circumstances to define him. There is one particular line from that film that has stayed with me for years. The character Red describes Andy's escape by saying that Andy crawled through a tunnel of filth and emerged on the other side smelling like a rose. That vivid image captures the essence of transformation. It reminds us that the journey toward renewal often requires walking through the most unpleasant and uncomfortable circumstances imaginable.

My own life has included several transformations. Some of them emerged during the darkest periods I have experienced. Those moments were not pleasant, and in truth, some of them felt deeply uncomfortable and painful at the time. Yet the strange paradox of transformation is that the most difficult seasons of life often produce the most meaningful growth. The experiences that feel the most discouraging while they are happening can eventually become the very moments that shape who we are meant to become.

Transformation has a way of humbling a person. When life pushes us into situations that challenge our identity or our sense of direction, we are forced to examine ourselves honestly. That process reveals truths about our character that might otherwise remain hidden. It strips away illusions and exposes the core of who we really are. In that sense, transformation acts like a mirror, reflecting both our weaknesses and our potential.

At the same time, transformation has a remarkable ability to renew a person. When someone passes through a difficult season and emerges on the other side, they rarely remain the same. Something inside them has shifted. Their perspective has broadened. Their understanding of themselves and the world has deepened. The person who steps forward after such an experience often carries a sense of clarity that did not exist before.

Every genuine transformation involves change. Change requires letting go of the version of ourselves that once existed and embracing the person we need to become. This process is rarely comfortable because it asks us to release familiar habits, identities, and expectations. Yet it is also the doorway through which growth occurs.

Nature itself offers countless examples of transformation. A caterpillar entering a cocoon does not simply grow larger or stronger. It undergoes a complete metamorphosis. The creature that emerges from that cocoon is fundamentally different from the one that entered it. Butterflies and many other animals experience this kind of dramatic change as part of their natural life cycle. Their transformation illustrates how renewal is woven into the fabric of the natural world.

Human transformation sometimes follows a similar pattern. There are seasons when growth requires solitude or reflection. Moments of seclusion can create the quiet space necessary for someone to reconnect with their own thoughts and emotions. During those periods, a person often rediscovers parts of themselves that had been buried beneath the noise and pressure of everyday life.

The stories presented in this book reflect that process. Each chapter reveals individuals who encountered life-altering circumstances that forced them to confront difficult realities. Many of those stories include pain, uncertainty, and heartbreak. Yet within those struggles lies the beginning of transformation. The people in these pages did not simply endure hardship. They allowed those experiences to reshape them into stronger and more purposeful individuals.

This collection of stories stands as a celebration of redemption. It demonstrates that transformation is not limited to a select few extraordinary individuals. It is a possibility available to anyone who is willing to face adversity with courage and honesty. The journeys described here reveal both the emotional weight of struggle and the remarkable strength that emerges when people refuse to surrender to despair.

For readers who may currently find themselves in the middle of their own difficult season, these stories offer encouragement. Transformation often begins quietly, long before we recognize that it is happening. The uncertainty you feel today may be the first step toward becoming the person you were meant to be.

I invite you to move through these stories with an open mind and heart. Within them, you will find examples of resilience, redemption, and personal renewal. More importantly, you may discover the inspiration needed to recognize the transformation unfolding in your own life.

Enjoy the stories.

Trunnis Goggins II

U.S. Navy veteran, author, educator, consultant, and the visionary behind the acclaimed "Stories of" book series.

https://4ps-group.com/

https://veritaspublishinghouse.com/

THE STORY OF BARNABY & ANGELA GUIRGUIS-HOWARTH

THE STRENGTH INSIDE IS ENOUGH

A Story of Confirmation, Not Miracle

My story of miraculous transformation is not entirely miraculous, nor is it truly a dramatic transformation. Instead, it is more accurately a confirmation, an affirmation of something that often lies quietly within each of us until life demands that we recognize it. It is the confirmation that the strength and resilience we carry inside ourselves are already enough to face the challenges life places before us. Sometimes that realization arrives gently through reflection. Other times it appears suddenly, in the middle of fear, uncertainty, or loss, forcing us to see clearly what had always been present but unrecognized. My story belongs to the latter.

Yet even describing it as *"my story"* does not feel entirely accurate. The heart of this story belongs to my late wife, Angela Guirguis-Howarth, **"Angel"**, as those closest to her lovingly called her. Today, she rests beside her father in heaven after a courageous journey through breast cancer. Her life, her courage, and her quiet determination shaped the lessons that follow far more than anything I experienced alone. While I may be the one telling the story, it is her spirit that carries its meaning.

There is one moment I will never forget. It is etched permanently into my memory the moment when I watched the expression in Angel's eyes change. Before that moment, I could see the weight of uncertainty pressing on her, the quiet fear that what she possessed internally might not be enough to face a potentially terminal diagnosis. The room seemed to hold a kind of heavy stillness, as though time itself had paused to witness the gravity of the moment. Then something shifted. It was subtle, almost imperceptible at first, but unmistakable once it appeared. The uncertainty gave way to resolve, and the softness in her eyes transformed into the strength of a lion.

That realization, what I often describe as the moment when *"the penny dropped,"* changed everything. Angel suddenly understood that she did not need to search outside herself for the strength to endure what lay ahead. She already possessed it. It had been there all along, quietly waiting beneath the fear and uncertainty that so often accompany life's most difficult moments. When she recognized that truth, a profound calm replaced the anxiety that had filled the room. Her posture straightened, her breathing steadied, and the quiet determination in her eyes communicated a powerful message: she was ready.

In many ways, Angela's experience mirrored a lesson I had been learning throughout my own life long before we met. When I was fourteen years old, I was diagnosed with type 1 diabetes, a diagnosis that forced me to confront adversity at an early age. Managing the condition required discipline, patience, and a willingness to accept responsibility for my health every single day. Yet the diagnosis did not define the limits of my life. Instead, it became the beginning of a journey that would test and ultimately confirm the strength that existed within me.

Over the years, that journey took me to places I never imagined possible. I played a season in the Australian Football League (AFL) as a professional athlete, competing at the highest level of the sport I loved. I wrote a book, telling stories that reflected lessons learned along the way. I filmed nineteen documentaries, exploring stories of perseverance and human potential. I climbed Mount Kilimanjaro, trekked across the challenging terrain of the Kokoda Track, and eventually returned to football to play my one-hundredth game for my local club, a moment that symbolized both persistence and personal redemption.

These experiences did not make me extraordinary. Rather, they repeatedly confirmed something simple yet powerful: the resilience we need to face life's challenges is already within us. Each obstacle merely reveals what was there all along. Because of those experiences, I felt that when Angel received her diagnosis of secondary breast cancer just after we had spoken with the priest of her church about marrying in the Coptic Church, I had at least some perspective to offer. I had walked through my own share of adversity, and I believed deeply that the strength required to endure hardship is something every person carries inside themselves.

Still, there is a difference between believing in resilience as an idea and witnessing it unfold in someone you love. Watching Angel step into her strength transformed my understanding of courage. Her quiet resolve, her unwavering faith, and her willingness to face the unknown with dignity became a living reminder that resilience is not something granted only to a few extraordinary individuals. It is a human capacity, one that emerges when we recognize that the resources we need to endure already exist within us.

Angela's journey did not begin with a miracle, nor did it rely on one. Instead, it began with a realization: that the strength required to face life's greatest trials was already present within her heart.

In many ways, the simple fact that Angela and I lived long enough to find each other felt miraculous in itself. Our lives had already been shaped by experiences that easily could have ended very differently. Before we ever met, both of us had already stared into the face of mortality and learned what it meant to keep moving forward when circumstances suggested we should not. Those experiences did not make us extraordinary; rather, they revealed how fragile life can be and how remarkable it is when we are given the opportunity to continue living it. Looking back, it is impossible not to see those earlier trials as quiet stepping stones that eventually led us to one another.

When I was twenty-five years old, my life changed in an instant during an alcohol-fueled gang attack. What began as a chaotic confrontation quickly escalated into violence that left me critically injured. During the assault, my basilar artery was torn, a catastrophic injury that most people never survive. The basilar artery is the single vessel responsible for carrying blood from the body to the brain, and even minor damage to it carries an extraordinarily high fatality rate. Medical statistics suggest that when the artery is damaged, there is roughly a 96 percent chance of death. In my case, it was not merely damaged; it was completely torn.

The hours that followed were filled with uncertainty and fear. I was placed on life-support and remained there for four days while doctors worked to stabilize my condition. My family and friends were called to the hospital, many of them arriving with the painful understanding that they might be saying goodbye. My parents were quietly informed by the medical staff that they might eventually face the unimaginable decision of whether to turn off the machines keeping their son alive. Hospitals have a way of amplifying both hope and despair at the same time—the sterile smell of antiseptic, the quiet hum of machines, and the hushed conversations in hallways create an atmosphere where every moment feels heavy with possibility.

Seven days after the attack, something unexpected happened: I regained consciousness. For many people, waking up after such an ordeal would represent the end of the struggle. For me, it was only the beginning. Surviving the stroke, as it turned out, was the easy part. The damage caused by the torn artery had effectively erased the neurological pathways that had developed between my brain and the left side of my body during the first twenty-five years of my life. Signals that once moved effortlessly through my nervous system were suddenly gone. My brain no longer knew how to communicate with half of my body.

In practical terms, this meant that I would have to relearn how to use the entire left side of my body from the beginning. Simple actions that most people perform without thinking, lifting an arm, standing upright, and taking a step, became monumental tasks. Rehabilitation required patience, persistence, and an acceptance that progress would come slowly, often measured in inches rather than miles. In many ways, it felt as though I had been returned to the physical state of a newborn child, forced to rebuild movement and coordination piece by piece. Every small victory, wiggling a finger, shifting weight onto my leg, taking a single step, became a reminder that recovery was possible.

Angela's story carried its own quiet strength long before our paths crossed. Years before we met, she had faced her first breast cancer scare while living in Australia. At the time, she was in a relationship with someone who ultimately could not handle the emotional weight of the diagnosis. When confronted with the reality of serious illness, he chose to walk away, leaving Angela to face the uncertainty of treatment alone. Experiences like that reveal a great deal about both vulnerability and resilience. In Angela's case, it revealed just how strong she truly was.

Angela came from a proud Egyptian family, and through her, I learned many cultural perspectives that I found both fascinating and deeply meaningful. One story in particular has always stayed with me. When she received her first diagnosis, Angela made a decision that demonstrated both courage and compassion. She believed that her mother, someone she loved deeply, might struggle to cope with the emotional impact of the news. Rather than risk placing that burden on her family, Angela quietly chose to handle the situation on her own.

To do this, she moved from Sydney to Melbourne so she could undergo treatment privately. During that time, she lived entirely by herself while navigating the physical and emotional challenges of cancer treatment. Imagine the quiet strength required to make such a choice: leaving behind the comfort of family, settling into a new city, and attending medical appointments alone, all while carrying the weight of a life-altering diagnosis. Angela rarely spoke about those months in dramatic terms, but the story revealed the depth of her character. She was not only resilient but also fiercely protective of the people she loved.

For my Australian friends, particularly those who might be reading this and thinking, *"You can't put that in a book; her mum might find out!"* There is a twist to the story that still makes me smile. During Angela's second breast cancer journey, her mother quietly pulled me aside for a conversation. Her expression carried the calm certainty of someone who had been observing more than she had revealed.

With a gentle voice and a knowing smile, she said something that caught me completely off guard: *"I know Angela had cancer before. She thought I didn't, but I knew all along."*

In that moment, I realized something profound about families and love. Sometimes the people closest to us understand far more than we believe they do. Angela had tried to protect her mother from worry, believing she was shielding her from pain. Yet her mother, in her own quiet way, had already seen the truth and carried that knowledge silently out of love for her daughter. It was another reminder that strength and resilience often run through families in ways that are both subtle and powerful.

When I reflect on these stories now, the stroke that nearly ended my life and Angela's solitary battle with cancer before we ever met, I cannot help but see them as parallel journeys. Each of us had already walked through circumstances that tested our endurance and forced us to discover inner strength. Perhaps that is why, when our paths finally crossed, we recognized something familiar in one another: the quiet understanding that surviving adversity does not make a person invincible, but it does reveal the remarkable resilience that already lives within us.

When Our Paths Finally Crossed

The circumstances that eventually brought Angela and me together were surprisingly ordinary, yet looking back, they carried a quiet sense of inevitability. I had met a young couple, Sarah and Tom, through a former girlfriend. One evening, the four of us went out for dinner, and what began as a casual meal quickly turned into an enjoyable evening filled with conversation and laughter. Sarah and Tom were the kind of people who were easy to be around, warm, relaxed, and the sort of company that makes hours pass almost unnoticed. By the end of the night, the three of us realized we had genuinely enjoyed each other's company, so we exchanged phone numbers with the casual promise that we should all catch up again sometime.

As often happens in busy lives, however, time slipped away. Weeks passed, and then months, without any of us actually reaching out. The intention to reconnect remained somewhere in the background, but everyday responsibilities gradually pushed it aside. Then, completely out of the blue, I received a text message from Sarah. The message was short and direct: *"I have a friend I want to set you up with."*

Now, I had seen enough horror movies to know that sentences like that can be the beginning of something unpredictable. Blind dates have a reputation for going either incredibly well or spectacularly wrong. For a moment, I hesitated, wondering what kind of situation I might be walking into. Eventually, curiosity won out over caution. I shrugged to myself and thought, What the hell—I'll give it a crack.

Not long afterward, Sarah and Tom introduced me to Angela Guirguis. Our first outing together was to the Sydney Opera House, where we attended a presentation featuring the National Geographic Wildlife Photographer of the Year exhibition. Even the setting itself felt remarkable. The Opera House stood illuminated against the darkening sky, its distinctive sails glowing softly above the harbor. Tourists and locals moved through the plaza in small clusters, their voices blending with the distant sounds of the water and city traffic. It was the kind of place that naturally made the evening feel a little more significant than a typical first meeting.

Angela, however, proved to be something of a tough nut to crack. She carried herself with a quiet reserve that suggested both shyness and caution. At first, she seemed a little nervous, carefully choosing her words and offering small smiles that hinted at her personality without fully revealing it. Yet there was something immediately captivating about her. She was distractingly beautiful in a way that was not simply physical but also deeply human, her warmth toward the people around her, the way her eyes softened when she spoke about family and friends, and the gentle happiness that seemed to sit just beneath her quiet demeanor.

As the evening unfolded, it became clear that she possessed a naturally kind spirit. Angela spoke about her family with affection and about her friends with loyalty, revealing the kind of values that tell you far more about a person than surface-level conversation ever could. The atmosphere between us remained relaxed, and although she was reserved, the overall vibe was undeniably positive. I left the Opera House that night with the sense that I had just met someone genuinely special.

About a week later, I decided to invite Angela out again. This time, I chose a jazz club in Sydney for our date. In truth, jazz music had never been my favorite genre. My selection of the venue had less to do with my musical tastes and more to do with the image I hoped to project. I wanted to appear cultured, intellectual, classy, and perhaps even a little emotionally intelligent. Whether or not I successfully achieved that impression is another matter entirely.

The jazz club itself was dimly lit, with small round tables scattered across the room and candles flickering softly in glass holders. The musicians played beneath warm stage lights, their instruments weaving together smooth, improvisational melodies that floated through the smoky air. Angela and I sat close together, sipping red wine while the music filled the space around us. Candlelight danced across the table as we began trading stories about our lives, our families, and the experiences that had shaped us.

As the night continued, something subtle began to shift between us. The conversation grew easier, deeper, and more natural with each passing hour. It felt as though we were gradually discovering a shared rhythm, each of us offering pieces of our lives while the other listened with genuine interest. The longer we sat there talking, the more it seemed that we were catching what the other was pitching, so to speak. The connection was not loud or dramatic; rather, it was quiet and steady, building slowly beneath the surface of our conversation.

Much of what I understood about how to treat a woman came from the men in my family, particularly my father and my grandfather. Both of them were old-school gentlemen who believed deeply in the importance of respect and courtesy. Growing up, I watched the way they interacted with the women in our family, and those examples shaped my own sense of what it meant to be a man. Simple gestures such as opening doors, pulling out chairs, and paying for dinner were not seen as grand acts but as natural expressions of appreciation and care.

So on that evening with Angela, I followed the habits I had learned from them. I opened doors, pulled out her chair, and covered the cost of our drinks. In modern Australian culture, those gestures can sometimes be met with skepticism or even a playful punch in the arm from someone who insists they can take care of themselves. But Angela came from a different cultural background, one shaped by Egyptian traditions where such gestures of chivalry were noticed and appreciated. Rather than appearing outdated, they seemed to resonate with her in a meaningful way.

By the time we said goodbye that night, there was very little doubt in my mind that we would see each other again.

After pretending to be a jazz enthusiast on our first official date, I decided that our second outing should reflect something that was authentically me. Surfing had always been a natural part of my life, so I invited Angela to join my brother Adam and me at the beach for a morning in the water. Sarah and Tom happened to live nearby, so we borrowed one of their wetsuits for Angela to wear before heading down to the sand.

The beach that day was bright and breezy, with waves rolling steadily toward the shore and the salty air carrying the sound of seabirds overhead. Adam was already waiting for us when we arrived, standing with his surfboard planted in the sand. After introducing the two of them, he pulled me aside with the unmistakable grin of a brother who had just noticed something amusing.

Leaning close so Angela could not hear, he whispered quietly in my ear, *"Does your girl know she's got her wetsuit on backwards?"*

I glanced over at Angela and realized immediately that he was right. The zipper was sitting awkwardly in the front, and the seams clearly did not belong where they were. For a moment, I considered telling her, but I also knew how nervous she had been about meeting my brother on only our second date. Angela cared deeply about what people thought of her, and I could easily imagine how embarrassed she might feel if the mistake were pointed out.

So I made a quick decision: I said nothing.

Instead, we headed into the water and spent the morning enjoying the surf together. Angela laughed as she tried to balance on the board, occasionally tumbling into the waves before climbing back up again with determination. The wetsuit may have been on backwards, but it did nothing to dampen the joy of the moment. We shared an easy, carefree time in the ocean, and by the time we returned to the shore, the early awkwardness of our second meeting had melted away.

It was around that time that things between us began to grow more serious. What had started as casual outings and lighthearted conversations slowly evolved into something deeper. The connection we had begun discovering in small moments during candlelit conversations and early mornings at the beach was gradually becoming something far more meaningful.

Returning to Faith and Finding Community

Angela's family was devout Coptic Christians. Before meeting her, I knew almost nothing about the Coptic faith. My understanding of Christianity had been shaped loosely by my own background as a non-practicing Anglican Australian, and although faith had always been present somewhere in the background of my life, it had never been something I studied closely. Yet the more time I spent with Angela and her family, the more I noticed something that quietly impressed me. The people around her seemed deeply motivated by their faith to be good, compassionate human beings. Their belief system was not simply a ritual practiced on Sundays. It was a guiding force that shaped how they treated others, how they carried themselves, and how they approached the world. Even though I did not fully understand the theology behind it, I respected the spirit of it enormously.

Angela eventually confided that she felt she had, in her words, *"strayed from the flock."* She explained that she had not been attending church as regularly as she once had. Much of that distance had come from the secret she believed she was carrying alone about her earlier cancer diagnosis. She had convinced herself that if she returned to church regularly, her mother might somehow discover the truth about what she had gone through. That quiet burden had created a kind of emotional distance between Angela and the spiritual community that had once been central to her life.

When she shared that with me, the solution seemed simple from my perspective. I told her that if she felt disconnected from something meaningful, then the answer was not to stay away from it. The answer was to return to it. I suggested that we simply go back to church together.

From that point forward, Angela and I began attending Saint George Coptic Orthodox Church in Kensington every Sunday. The church itself carried a sense of history and devotion that could be felt the moment you stepped inside. Sunlight filtered through the windows, casting warm reflections across the wooden pews and the ornate icons that lined the walls. The scent of incense lingered gently in the air as parishioners gathered quietly before the service. At first, I felt like an outsider stepping into an unfamiliar world, but that feeling did not last long.

Week by week, we began to know the other parishioners and the priests of the church. After each mass, the congregation would gather for coffee and conversation. Families stood together in small groups, friends greeted one another warmly, and laughter mixed with thoughtful discussion about life, faith, and everyday struggles. What struck me most was the authenticity of those interactions. The kindness that people extended to one another did not feel forced or performative. It felt genuine.

Those moments after mass often reminded me of being at my local football club, the Pennant Hills Demons. At the footy club, people show up for one another because they belong to the same team. At Saint George, the sense of belonging felt very similar. People cared about each other's lives. They asked real questions and listened to real answers. I always felt as though Angela and I were part of something larger than ourselves, something that sincerely wanted the best for both of us. The conversations were real, and the support we received was tangible. I consistently left the church with the feeling that we were respected, supported, and loved.

Whether it was because of reconnecting with the church or simply the natural evolution of our relationship, Angela and I began to flourish together during that time. Our connection deepened in ways that were difficult to describe but easy to feel. We understood each other at a level that went beyond surface conversation. Both of us had experienced significant challenges in our lives before we met, and perhaps that shared history created a bond that allowed us to appreciate each other in a unique way.

It often felt as though we were two pieces of a puzzle that had somehow found their way together. Angela balanced qualities in me that I did not even realize needed balancing. In many ways, we were the yin to each other's yang. There was a sense that each of us filled spaces in the other's life that had previously been empty. Given that we were both in our mid-thirties and neither of us was getting any younger, it did not take very long before conversations about the future naturally began to include the possibility of marriage.

Around this time, I had also developed a friendship with one of the priests at the church, Father Matthew. Over time, we began meeting regularly for coffee. Those meetings often included discussions about football, everyday life, and occasionally deeper conversations about faith and purpose. Father Matthew had a calm and thoughtful presence that made people feel comfortable around him. Much like the atmosphere I felt within the church community itself, every interaction with him seemed to revolve around care, kindness, and respect.

Because Angela and I had begun discussing marriage seriously, I eventually decided to ask Father Matthew a practical question. I explained that I was a non-practicing Anglican Australian and asked him what would be required for me to marry a Coptic woman in the Coptic Church. His response was clear and direct. As things stood, it would not be possible.

In the Coptic Orthodox tradition, both individuals who are getting married in the church must be members of the Coptic faith. Father Matthew explained that if Angela and I truly wanted to marry within the church, I would need to become part of that faith community myself. The path forward, he told me, would involve baptism and learning more about the Coptic tradition.

He outlined a process that would involve three learning sessions with him at the church. These meetings would help me understand the history, beliefs, and practices of the Coptic Orthodox Church before moving forward with baptism. Without hesitation, we began organizing those sessions. Angela and I were excited about the possibility of marrying in the very church her grandfather had helped build with his own hands. That history gave the place an even deeper significance for her family, and the idea of honoring that legacy felt profoundly meaningful.

Everything seemed to be falling into place. Plans were beginning to form, and the future appeared full of promise. Then, quite suddenly, an unexpected event disrupted our carefully unfolding path.

Angela had been closing a gate one day when she experienced a sharp and painful injury that resulted in a broken rib. The pain was severe enough that she had to be taken to the hospital. What initially appeared to be a simple accident would soon reveal itself to be something far more serious than anyone could have anticipated.

A Breast Cancer Diagnosis Begins Something Unexpected

Some moments in life divide time into two distinct parts. There is life before the moment and life after it. Angela's breast cancer diagnosis was one of those moments. What began as an ordinary day quickly unfolded into a turning point that would reshape our lives in ways neither of us could have imagined.

When I received a text message from Angela telling me she had been taken to the hospital, I felt an immediate rush of concern, but I did not yet grasp the seriousness of the situation. Injuries happen. People go to hospitals for many reasons that ultimately turn out to be minor. As I made my way there, my mind moved through a range of possibilities, none of which prepared me for what I was about to hear.

When I arrived at the hospital, Angela's sister's mother-in-law greeted me in the hallway and offered to walk me to Angela's room. That detail alone gave me a small measure of reassurance. I remember thinking that if the situation were truly difficult, Angela's own mother would probably have been there to meet me. The hospital corridors were quiet and sterile, the air filled with the faint smell of disinfectants. Nurses moved past us with calm efficiency while distant monitors beeped rhythmically behind closed doors.

When I stepped into Angela's room, however, the atmosphere immediately felt different. Angela was sitting upright in the hospital bed, and the expression on her face told me everything I needed to know before she even spoke. Her eyes were serious in a way I had never seen before. The warm, gentle smile that usually greeted me was absent, replaced by a look that carried fear and exhaustion.

When she told me the diagnosis, I understood instantly why she looked the way she did. Angela had been diagnosed with stage four breast cancer. The broken rib that had sent her to the hospital was not simply the result of a small accident while closing the gate at our apartment complex. The cancer had spread into her bones and weakened them to the point that even a routine movement could cause a fracture.

The words felt heavy in the room as they settled between us. The diagnosis sounded alarming, and Angela looked frightened in a way that made my chest tighten. In moments like that, however, something instinctive takes over. I had been raised in an environment where certain values were deeply ingrained. My family had taught me that when someone you love is struggling, you do not pause to consider your own needs or fears. Your role becomes clear. You show up for them.

So, I pushed my own shock aside and focused entirely on Angela. I told her that everything would be fine and that I was going to be there for her no matter what lay ahead. I reassured her that the conversations we had been having about marriage were still absolutely solid, assuming, of course, that the doctors approved and that her health allowed it. My intention was simple. I wanted her to know that nothing about this diagnosis changed the way I felt about her or the future I hoped we would share.

For a moment, the reassurance seemed to calm her. Her shoulders relaxed slightly, and the tension in her face softened. Then she grew serious again. The next thing she said would shake me in a way I did not expect.

She looked at me and said quietly, *"You can't tell my mother."*

At first, I thought I must have misunderstood her. The statement seemed so unexpected that my mind struggled to process it. My immediate assumption was that the words had come from a place of shock or emotional overwhelm. After all, Angela had just received devastating news. It would have been completely understandable if her thoughts were scattered or if she had spoken impulsively in the heat of the moment.

I believed that once the initial shock faded and she had time to think clearly, she would recognize how unrealistic the request sounded. Telling a daughter's mother about a life-threatening illness felt like the most natural step imaginable.

Yet it quickly became clear that Angela was not speaking impulsively. She was serious.

What I initially thought would be a brief moment of confusion eventually grew into a disagreement that lasted for weeks after her diagnosis. Angela was determined that her mother should not know. She believed she was protecting her from pain and worry, just as she had attempted to do during her earlier cancer scare.

While Angela and I discussed this difficult topic, I made one decision immediately. I told her that the first people I needed to call were my own parents. Within a short time, they arrived at the hospital to be with us. Like me, they were surprised to discover that Angela's mother was not there. In situations like this, parents naturally expect to be present for their children.

Despite our confusion, we all understood something important. The moment did not belong to us. It belonged to Angela.

Whatever decisions needed to be made, ultimately, had to respect what she was experiencing and what she believed she needed. So rather than continuing to debate the issue right then, we set it aside temporarily. There would be time to address it later.

Instead, we focused on being present with her. We sat together in that hospital room, talking quietly about the road ahead. The atmosphere carried a mixture of uncertainty and determination. None of us truly felt strong in that moment, but we did our best to act as though we were. Sometimes strength begins not with confidence but simply with the decision to remain standing beside someone when life suddenly becomes frightening and uncertain.

Together in Holy Matrimony

With only one thought in my mind, I focused on helping Angela feel safe. Everything else seemed secondary. The future felt uncertain, but there was one thing I believed strongly. If Angela had something beautiful to look forward to, it might give her strength during the frightening weeks ahead. Because of that, I decided we would keep moving forward with our plans to get married.

I still had the three learning sessions scheduled with Father Matthew as part of the process for my baptism into the Coptic Orthodox Church. After explaining Angela's diagnosis to him, I told him that I wanted to continue with the process exactly as planned. The idea of stepping back or delaying anything felt wrong. If anything, Angela's illness made the commitment feel even more meaningful.

When I arrived at the church for the first learning session, Father Matthew greeted me warmly and handed me a Bible. What followed was an intense ninety minutes of teaching. He spoke about the foundations of the Coptic faith, the meaning of baptism, and the responsibilities that came with becoming part of the church community. His explanations were thoughtful and detailed, and I tried my best to absorb everything he was sharing.

By the time the lesson ended, my head felt completely full. I was mentally exhausted and half-jokingly asked him if that had only been the first of the three learning sessions.

Father Matthew smiled and responded calmly. *"No. I combined all three into one lesson, given Angela's health. We are finished. You can be baptized tomorrow if you would like."*

His kindness in that moment meant more than I could properly express. He had recognized the urgency of our situation and quietly adjusted the process to help us move forward.

I organized the baptism for the following weekend at Saint George Church. What unfolded that day was a mixture of joy, tension, and awkwardness that none of us could fully escape. If awkwardness were a strawberry, we all would have been drinking a lot of smoothies that morning.

I invited my entire family, along with a couple of former teammates from my football days, who I knew were spiritually minded. Sarah and Tom were also there. Angela invited her family as well. However, I had quietly instructed my own friends and family that we were not to reveal Angela's cancer diagnosis to her mother. Keeping that secret in a room filled with people who cared deeply about her created an emotional tension that was almost impossible to ignore. Even saying this now makes me wince a little. It felt wrong in many ways, yet at the time, we believed we were honoring Angela's wishes.

The ceremony itself was beautiful. Wearing the traditional white robe, I stepped into the baptismal waters inside the church. The cool water surrounded me as the priest completed the ritual that formally welcomed me into the Coptic Orthodox faith. The moment carried a deep sense of symbolism and commitment.

Thankfully, the tension in the room was broken by an unexpected moment of humor. As I stepped out of the water, my young nephew AJ loudly announced to his father that he could see Uncle Barns' underwear. The innocent observation echoed through the room and immediately caused laughter to ripple through the congregation. In a moment that could have felt overly serious, a child's honesty brought everyone back to earth.

With the baptism complete, I was officially a Coptic Christian. Angela and I quickly set our wedding date so that amid the fear and uncertainty surrounding her illness, she would have something hopeful to anticipate.

During this time, I was spending a great deal of time with Angela's Egyptian friends and family. I grew particularly close to many of them. What struck me most about the entire community was the genuine kindness they extended toward one another. They were generous with their time, their encouragement, and their support. I felt welcomed into their circle in a way that made me feel as though I truly belonged.

That sense of belonging grew even stronger one day when Father Matthew called me unexpectedly. He asked if I would like to serve as a Deacon during the Easter Sunday service.

At the time, I did not fully grasp what a significant honor this was. Easter Sunday is the holiest day in the Coptic calendar, and being invited by a priest to serve as a Deacon during that service is a remarkable sign of trust and respect. Unfortunately, my lack of understanding led me to treat the occasion a little too casually.

When I arrived at the church that morning, I was wearing my Sydney Swans shirt and enthusiastically waving my GoPro camera around like a tourist visiting Bondi Beach for the first time. I recorded everything I could see, including scenes behind the altar that in hindsight probably bordered on sacrilegious. At the time, I was simply excited to capture the moment, unaware of how informal my behavior might have appeared.

Despite my enthusiastic approach, I continued serving as a Deacon many times after that first experience. I participated in services at several churches and even served during a mass led by a Bishop visiting Sydney from the Red Sea region. That particular service was conducted in the Egyptian-speaking congregation, which made the experience both humbling and slightly confusing. Although I understood none of the language being spoken, the atmosphere made it clear that the occasion was deeply meaningful.

As the weeks passed, Angela and I grew closer than ever. Our relationship had always been strong, but facing such difficult circumstances together seemed to deepen our bond even further. Yet one issue continued to weigh heavily on my mind. Angela still refused to tell her mother about the cancer diagnosis.

The secrecy began to trouble me deeply. I could not stop thinking about the potential consequences if the worst-case scenario occurred. After everything we had experienced together, the thought of losing Angela was terrifying enough. The idea that her mother might learn about the illness only after something tragic happened felt unbearable.

Eventually, I shared that concern openly with Angela. I explained that if something terrible were to happen and her mother later discovered the truth, there would only be one person she would come looking for. That person would be me.

As I explained my reasoning, I saw a shift in Angela's expression. It was as though a realization had finally settled into place. The weight of what I was saying made sense to her.

Not long after that conversation, we went together to tell her mother the truth.

Her mother responded exactly as any loving parent would. The news made her emotional and deeply saddened for her daughter. Yet almost immediately she shifted into protective mode. She began doing all the things strong mothers instinctively do. She cooked meals, prepared baths, attended medical appointments, and surrounded Angela with care and attention.

With that secret finally lifted from our shoulders, both Angela and I felt an enormous sense of relief. The emotional tension that had hovered over us for weeks began to fade. With clearer minds and lighter hearts, we threw ourselves into planning our wedding.

Father Matthew would conduct the ceremony inside Saint George Coptic Orthodox Church. After the ceremony, the wedding party would travel to the Opera Bar in Sydney for photographs overlooking the harbor. From there, we would move to the Royal Botanic Gardens, where our reception would take place beneath the evening sky.

The wedding night itself was extraordinary. It was filled with happiness, laughter, and an atmosphere of warmth that surrounded everyone present. So many people went out of their way to help us that it almost feels dangerous to list them for fear of leaving someone out. Still, several gestures stand out clearly in my memory.

Father Matthew moved mountains to expedite my baptism and graciously arranged the ceremony at Saint George Church. My old football teammate, Luke Turner, and his wife, Lauren, generously handled our wedding photography. Our friend Mary Andrawis Megalaa served as the master of ceremonies for the reception. Emmanuel Kelly performed music during the celebration and filled the evening with his powerful voice.

Ray and Marg Miles arranged a beautiful hotel room at the InterContinental for Angela and me for our wedding night. Ash Mansour brought his classic wedding cars out of retirement to transport the wedding party. Mary Ibrahim drove her Mini as the getaway car that carried Angela and me to the hotel after the reception. Angela's Uncle Adel traveled all the way from Dallas to join the celebration. Lillian Botros organized the flowers that decorated the ceremony and reception.

My brothers Adam and Lachlan stood proudly beside me as my best men. My parents, Ross and Denise, were there supporting us as they always had throughout my life.

At celebrations that revolve around a single person or couple, such as graduations, milestone birthdays, engagements, or weddings, I have often encouraged people to pause for a moment and quietly observe the room around them. When everyone gathers to celebrate you, it is worth taking a second to absorb the atmosphere.

That night I followed my own advice.

I stepped back for a moment and simply looked around the room. The reception hall glowed softly with warm lighting. Conversations filled the air while glasses clinked together in celebration. Guests had traveled from across Australia and even from overseas to be there with us.

Everywhere I looked, people were smiling.

At one point, my eyes landed on Angela and her mother standing together in the middle of the room. They were telling a story to one another and laughing uncontrollably, their arms wrapped around each other with pure affection.

In that moment, as I watched the two of them laughing together, I felt a sense of happiness so complete that it almost seemed impossible to describe.

I am almost certain that no man in the history of the world has ever felt happier than I did at that exact moment.

A Nineteen Leg Honeymoon

Not long before I met Angela, I had taken a leap that felt both exciting and uncertain. I had started a small business as a sole trader focused on keynote speaking, resilience coaching, and podcast hosting. The work revolved around telling stories of perseverance and helping others find strength through adversity. When Angela and I married, it occurred to me that this platform might allow us to do something unusual for our honeymoon. Rather than taking a short traditional trip, I decided to build speaking engagements and meetings into our travel schedule so that we could see the world together. In the end, that idea became a nineteen-leg international honeymoon.

One of the places Angela was most eager to visit was San Diego. Several members of her extended family lived there, including a cousin who served as the Chief Executive Officer of the Starlight Foundation. Angela had always spoken about her with a mixture of admiration and hesitation. When I asked her when the last time they had spoken was, she looked slightly uncomfortable and admitted that she had not reached out in quite some time.

Her explanation surprised me.

She said she felt hesitant to call because her cousin was so successful that it made her feel intimidated. Angela joked that her cousin was practically a celebrity and that she would probably be too busy to talk.

I told Angela that she was being ridiculous. Family was family, no matter how successful someone became. I asked her to pass me her phone. When she handed it over, I found her cousin's number and called it without hesitation.

The call was answered almost immediately. A cheerful voice greeted us with a bright American accent. She enthusiastically said hello and mentioned that she had not spoken to her cousin in ages. When I explained that it was actually me calling and introduced myself as Angela's husband, she burst into laughter. I briefly explained Angela's cancer situation, which she already knew about through other family members, and then asked if Angela and I could come and stay with them for a few days while we were traveling through the United States.

Her response was immediate and joyful. She told us we were welcome any time and that she would love to see Angela.

With that conversation, the American portion of our honeymoon was officially underway.

Angela seemed emboldened by the experience. The small moment of courage it took to reconnect with her cousin seemed to awaken something in her. Soon afterward, she reached out to another group of cousins who lived on the opposite side of the United States. She told me they probably would not be able to meet us because they had never been allowed to drive outside their neighborhood, let alone across the entire country.

What happened next surprised both of us. When the younger cousins asked their mother for permission to make the journey and explained that it was to see Angela, her response was immediate. Her concern melted into encouragement. She simply told them to drive carefully and assured them they absolutely could go.

When we finally arrived in San Diego, the warmth of Angela's family surrounded us immediately. I even managed to secure a keynote speaking opportunity at a local pub to help contribute toward the cost of the trip. Our extended family came along to support the event, and the experience became far more than just a professional engagement.

One of the most remarkable things about Egyptian culture is the way hospitality is expressed. Guests are not merely welcomed. They are embraced as though they have always belonged there. Meals were shared around large tables, conversations flowed easily, and laughter seemed to fill every corner of the house. Leaving San Diego was genuinely difficult because of how loved we felt during our time there.

Fortunately, our next destination helped soften the emotional blow of departure. Our honeymoon itinerary included a stop at Disneyland in California.

Before reaching Disneyland, however, we made a brief stop at a Pancake Factory restaurant in Los Angeles. Angela mentioned casually that a few members of her family might meet us there. When we walked inside the restaurant, I quickly realized that Angela and I had very different definitions of the word "few."

There were roughly thirty-five people waiting to greet us.

Some of them had driven for several hours just to see Angela during our short visit. As I watched cousins, uncles, and extended relatives crowd around her with smiles and hugs, I began to understand something about Angela that even she might not have fully recognized about herself. There was something within her that drew people in. Her warmth, her kindness, and her sincerity made people want to be around her.

Our visit to Disneyland felt almost surreal. As a child growing up in Australia, I had often dreamed about visiting the famous park. I had imagined seeing the Indiana Jones ride, standing in front of the Disney Castle, and watching the fireworks explode above the park at night. Experiencing those things in person was magical.

Yet the most extraordinary part of the trip had nothing to do with rides or fireworks. It was something far more subtle.

I began to notice a change in Angela.

One of her cousins had even booked a room at the Disneyland hotel where we were staying just so she could spend more time with Angela. As they laughed together and walked through the park, I watched Angela's face closely. The fear and desperation that had once filled her eyes had disappeared. In its place was something entirely different.

Confidence.

Pride.

Happiness.

Her cancer had not vanished. The diagnosis still existed. The treatments still lie ahead. Yet the helpless anxiety that had once surrounded her seemed to have evaporated. In its place was a quiet determination that suggested she had rediscovered her inner strength.

Our final stop in the United States took us to Dallas, where we visited Uncle Adel. He had flown all the way to Sydney to attend our wedding, and now we were able to return the visit. While in Dallas, we stayed with the Attala family, who welcomed us with the same warmth and generosity we had experienced throughout Angela's extended family.

I had always believed that I loved Angela deeply. Watching the way her cousins embraced her, however, made me realize that I might have some competition. Every person she encountered treated her with genuine affection. What struck me most was that their love did not feel like sympathy. It was not the gentle pity sometimes extended to someone facing illness.

It was genuine admiration.

Angela was adored because she was simply an extraordinary human being.

On our way back to Australia, we stopped briefly in Canada to visit members of my own family. We stayed with my aunt and uncle, along with my cousin, her husband, and their young daughter. My uncle had recently completed construction on several luxury cabins beside a river, and Angela and I became the very first guests to stay in them. The cabins were stunning, with heated concrete flooring and enormous windows that stretched from floor to ceiling and looked out across the water.

Canada provided several unforgettable moments. While driving along the freeway, we saw a bear lying peacefully in the sun on a concrete divider between lanes. My aunt organized a smoking ceremony in Banff, conducted by an Indigenous elder named Roland Rollinmud at a sacred site surrounded by towering mountains. Angela saw snow for the first time while we were attending a family dinner inside a beautiful log cabin home. The sight of snowflakes drifting gently outside the windows filled her with childlike excitement.

We also went bobsledding at the Canadian Olympic Park with some of my old friends and their children. The adrenaline of racing down the icy track left us laughing and breathless. During our time in Calgary, I gave another speech at a local pub, continuing the pattern of blending work with our adventure.

One particularly special moment occurred when an old friend named Mike Gretton came to see us. Mike and I had met years earlier on a Contiki tour in 1999, and he made the effort to visit while Angela and I were at the Olympic Park preparing for the bobsled ride. Moments like that reminded me how friendships formed decades earlier can still resurface unexpectedly.

Eventually, our honeymoon came to an end, and we returned to Australia. The reality of Angela's cancer treatment waited for us there. The hospital visits, the medical consultations, and the difficult conversations about treatment options could no longer be postponed.

Yet something had changed.

During the earlier stages of her diagnosis, I had been the one trying to reassure Angela. Now it seemed that our roles had quietly reversed. When I looked into her eyes, I saw a calm confidence that had not been there before. It was as though she was gently telling me that she appreciated everything I had done to support her.

The message in her eyes seemed to say something simple.

Thank you for helping me.

You can stand down now.

It is going to be alright.

I have this.

Angela Finds Her Strength Inside

Not long after we returned from North America, Angela and I were visiting her mother one evening. The atmosphere at the house had been calm and familiar, the kind of environment that normally helped Angela relax. Yet on that particular night, something seemed unsettled within her. She shifted constantly in her chair and could not find a comfortable position. The usual ease in her voice was gone. Even the small conversations that typically filled the room felt strained because it was obvious that she was uncomfortable.

Angela's mother noticed immediately that something was not right. Like many mothers who instinctively know when their child is struggling, she moved quickly into action. She suggested that Angela try taking a warm bath, hoping it might help ease whatever pain or tension she was feeling. The house filled with the quiet sounds of running water while Angela attempted to settle herself.

The bath did not help.

If anything, her discomfort intensified. Within a short time, it became clear that we were dealing with something more serious than simple restlessness or pain that could be soothed by warm water. The anxiety in the room grew quickly, and we made the decision to call an ambulance.

The paramedics arrived swiftly and transported Angela to Royal Prince Alfred Hospital. The drive there felt strangely quiet. The flashing lights reflected against the windows of the ambulance while the medical staff monitored her condition carefully. When we arrived, the emergency department moved quickly to conduct a series of scans and tests. Doctors and nurses spoke in calm professional tones as they worked, but the seriousness of the situation hung in the air.

After reviewing the initial scans, the medical team explained that Angela's symptoms appeared to be related to her cancer diagnosis. Because of this, they decided she would receive more specialized care at Chris O'Brien Lifehouse, a cancer treatment center located just across the road from the hospital.

Angela was transferred there shortly afterward.

As she was wheeled through the entrance of Lifehouse, the uncertainty surrounding her condition became almost tangible. The bright lights of the hospital corridors reflected against polished floors while medical staff moved with practiced efficiency around us. Despite the calm professionalism of the doctors and nurses, I could see fear returning to Angela's eyes. The strength and confidence that had begun to grow during our honeymoon seemed momentarily overshadowed by the anxiety of being back inside a hospital environment.

The doctors who spoke with us were kind and reassuring. Their words were carefully chosen and delivered with compassion. Yet I could not shake the feeling that the results they were presenting contained more troubling information than they were openly expressing. The tension in the room slowly built as we tried to understand the medical explanations being offered.

Eventually, one of the doctors entered Angela's room to deliver additional results. As she spoke, the medical terminology and cautious language made it difficult for us to fully grasp what was being communicated. Angela listened quietly at first, but it was obvious that the uncertainty was frustrating her.

Suddenly, something shifted.

Angela exploded into an angry outburst that caught everyone off guard. She began speaking to the doctor with an intensity that was far beyond anything I had ever seen from her. The words came quickly and sharply, driven by fear, frustration, and the emotional exhaustion that had been building for weeks. The verbal tirade was so forceful that it startled me. The doctor, understandably shaken by the confrontation, stepped out of the room and retreated toward her office.

Angela's face was tense and fierce. She was breathing heavily, like a lion that had just finished a hunt but still carried the energy of the chase within its body. The anger had not yet burned itself out.

Before anyone could react, Angela began pulling the medical tubes from her arms and stormed out into the hallway. She marched down the corridor toward the doctor's office, shouting loudly and demanding answers. The scene unfolded with chaotic intensity as nurses hurried after her in an attempt to calm the situation.

Eventually, with the help of several members of the nursing staff who were considerably stronger than I was, we managed to guide Angela back to her room. The emotional storm that had overtaken her slowly began to fade. It seemed as though the physical release of anger had exhausted her completely. Within a short time, she fell into a deep sleep.

Once Angela was resting, I slipped quietly out of the room and walked down the corridor toward the doctor's office. I wanted to make sure she was alright after the confrontation.

When I was allowed inside, the sight of her made me feel even more apologetic. She looked pale and shaken, as though she had just experienced something deeply unsettling. Her hands were trembling slightly, and her voice carried the faint unsteadiness of someone who had just endured an unexpected shock.

I apologized as sincerely as I could. I explained that Angela was overwhelmed and frightened, and that the outburst came from a place of fear rather than hostility. The doctor listened patiently and accepted the apology with professional grace.

After that conversation, I returned to Angela's room.

She slept through the rest of the night without disturbance. The following morning, she woke up calm and surprisingly unaware of the full intensity of the previous evening's events. Her memory of the outburst seemed vague and distant, as though it had occurred in a dream.

We continued with the routine of hospital life as though nothing unusual had happened.

Yet something about the environment at Chris O'Brien Lifehouse began to affect Angela in a remarkably positive way. The staff there approached their work with a kind of humanity that was deeply refreshing. Every nurse, doctor, and support worker entered the room with genuine warmth. They greeted Angela with smiles and engaged her in ordinary conversation.

They asked about her family. They complimented her clothing. They commented on the weather outside or shared small observations about the day. What stood out most was that they did not treat Angela as though she were defined by her illness.

There were no overly dramatic conversations about her potentially terminal diagnosis. There was no sense that she was being handled like a fragile charity case. Instead, she was treated simply as a person who deserved kindness, dignity, and respect.

Gradually, something inside Angela began to shift.

Over the course of the week she spent at Lifehouse, the fear that had clouded her spirit seemed to fade. The kindness surrounding her created space for something stronger to emerge. The hospital environment that could have easily reinforced despair instead became a place where Angela rediscovered her sense of self.

I will never forget the moment we finally left the hospital.

As we stepped through the large glass doors and onto the footpath outside, Angela paused for a moment. The sunlight reflected in her eyes as she looked ahead toward the street. When I studied her expression, I saw a look that was both calm and powerful.

Her eyes carried the strength of a lion.

The fear that had once lived there was gone. In its place was a quiet understanding that she could not control what might happen next. She did not know how long she had. None of us did.

But the message in her eyes was unmistakable.

She understood that everything she needed to face whatever lay ahead already existed within her.

Angela Leaves This Earth with a Smile on Her Face

Angela's belief in herself had changed dramatically during the final months of her life. The transformation was quiet but unmistakable. The fear that had once dominated her thoughts had been replaced by a calm sense of acceptance and inner strength. Unfortunately, the timing of this emotional shift coincided with a period when her physical health was declining rapidly. Each day seemed to bring new evidence that the cancer was gaining ground.

Eventually, Angela was moved into a hospice where she could receive specialized care during the final stage of her illness. Although the circumstances were heartbreaking, the environment surrounding her became one filled with compassion and tenderness. In many ways, it felt as though the kindness Angela had shown people throughout her life was now returning to her in a powerful and beautiful way.

The spiritual care she received was extraordinary. Priests from Saint George Coptic Orthodox Church visited regularly, offering prayers and comfort. Other priests from nearby churches also came to spend time with her. One particularly meaningful visit occurred when a Bishop who had traveled from the Red Sea region happened to be in Sydney again. After hearing about Angela's condition, the priests arranged for him to come to the hospice and pray with her.

Watching these moments unfold filled the room with a quiet sense of reverence. The prayers, the gentle voices, and the deep respect shown by the clergy created an atmosphere that felt sacred.

At one point, however, the spiritual care being offered to Angela nearly collided with a much more casual form of Australian family support.

One afternoon, I had asked my brother if he could bring a small amount of marijuana to the hospice. He kindly agreed, knowing it might help Angela find a little relief from the discomfort she was experiencing. The cannabis was sitting out on a table when suddenly someone down the hallway shouted that the priests were coming up in the elevator.

The realization hit me instantly.

I jumped up, grabbed the marijuana, and shoved it into a bag that I quickly placed inside a cupboard. After slamming the cupboard door shut, I paused for a moment and reopened it just to make sure nothing was sticking out. As soon as I cracked the door open, the smell poured out so strongly that it nearly knocked me backward.

Panic set in.

Thinking quickly, I grabbed several packets of instant coffee from a basket near the microwave, tore them open, and poured the coffee grounds into the bag in a desperate attempt to mask the smell. I closed the cupboard again and hoped with all my might that the priests would not decide to look inside.

Thankfully, they did not.

They entered the room quietly, greeted Angela gently, and began praying beside her bed. Their voices carried the calm rhythm of sacred words while the room fell into a peaceful silence. After finishing their prayers, they offered their blessings and left the room without the slightest hint of suspicion about what might be hidden in the cupboard.

Angela spent most of her time in the hospice under the influence of strong pain medication. The medication helped manage her physical suffering, but it also meant she drifted in and out of awareness throughout the day. Even so, I often felt that somewhere deep inside she sensed the presence of the people who came to visit her. Friends and family members regularly filled the room, each bringing their own stories, memories, and quiet expressions of love.

It felt as though the room itself had become a gathering place for gratitude.

On the day Angela passed away, the hospice room was filled with the gentle sounds of conversation and laughter. Friends and family were sharing stories about Angela's life. Some memories were funny, others emotional, but all of them reflected the impact she had made on the people around her.

At one point, my mother, who had once worked as a nurse, walked quietly over to me. She leaned close and whispered softly that she believed Angela had just passed.

Her words landed gently but carried enormous weight.

Moments later, the nursing staff entered the room and confirmed what my mother had sensed. Angela had peacefully left this earth.

It was one of the saddest moments of my life, yet at the same time, it was one of the moments I felt most proud of her.

When Angela had first received her diagnosis, she had doubted whether she possessed the strength to face what lay ahead. She believed the challenge might be more than she could handle.

Yet the woman who left this world had proven something extraordinary.

Angela had never held a job during the time we were together, which meant she spent many days at home while I went to work. Being alone during those long hours often weighed heavily on her emotions. There were several evenings when I returned home and found her visibly distressed.

When I asked her what was wrong on one particular day, she told me something that shook me deeply.

She said that earlier that day, she had considered taking her own life. The thought had crossed her mind while she was alone at home. The only reason she had decided not to act on that thought was that she was looking forward to my returning home that evening.

Moments like that revealed the depth of the emotional battles Angela fought quietly each day. Society often teaches us that strength must be measurable or repeatable to be considered real. People tend to associate resilience with visible accomplishments, physical endurance, or public achievements.

Yet I have never met anyone stronger or more resilient than Angela.

Her strength did not come from trophies, titles, or statistics. It came from the way she lived her life. Angela dedicated herself to caring for others. Every person she encountered was treated with kindness, respect, and genuine compassion. Her life was filled with countless small acts of goodness that often went unnoticed in the moment.

Over time, those small acts became seeds planted throughout the lives of the people she touched.

When Angela left this world, the room full of love surrounding her was the harvest of those seeds. The laughter, the tears, and the stories being shared were living proof of the impact she had made.

Even now, when I think back to that moment, I can almost feel her presence in the room. I imagine the warm smile that so often lit up her face. It feels as though that smile continues to exist somewhere beyond the physical world, quietly encouraging those of us she left behind.

In a strange and beautiful way, Angela's smile still makes me stronger.

BARNABY HOWARTH

Relatable Resilience Coach

Barnaby Howarth is a dynamic resilience coach and speaker dedicated to helping individuals and organizations move beyond setbacks and live with purpose and strength. With over a decade of experience, he empowers audiences to unlock their inner resilience and navigate life's challenges with confidence.

Drawing from his extraordinary life journey—including managing type 1 diabetes from age 14, playing for the Sydney Swans at 18, surviving a stroke at 25, and experiencing the loss of his spouse at 36—Barnaby delivers authentic, hard-earned insights that resonate deeply.

Specializing in resilience, motivation, mental health, and self-awareness, he combines powerful storytelling with practical strategies to inspire meaningful growth. Known for his positive energy, authenticity, and professionalism, Barnaby connects with diverse audiences—from schools to corporate teams and correctional facilities—helping people embrace change, build strength through adversity, and realize their full potential.

Connect with Barnaby

https://barnabyhowarth.com.au/

THE STORY OF DR. LISA YVETTE JONES

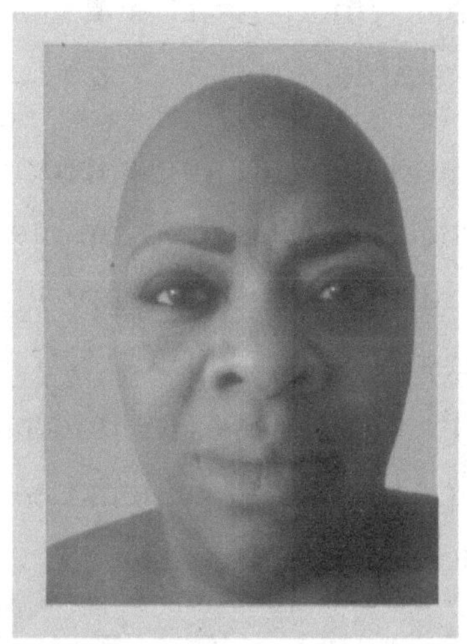

FROM CANCER TO COURAGEOUS, A LEADER'S S.U.C.C.E.S.S. JOURNEY TO LIVE!

This chapter serves as a beacon of hope and a practical guide for anyone grappling with the challenges of health crises, the power of leadership, one of the effects of obesity, and living a life of healing and wholeness. My personal journey, marked by a transformative struggle with obesity and a battle with stage 3 cervical cancer with no symptoms and two death sentences, underscores the profound impact my faith and that health can have on one's ability to lead well, look well, live well, and to love well. By sharing my story, I aim to illustrate that overcoming these obstacles is possible, emerging stronger and healthier, and truly leading by example.

The strategies and insights presented in this chapter are not merely theoretical; they are proven methods I employed to reclaim my health and enhance my life, personally and professionally. These Seven **S.U.C.C.ES.S.** Strategies focused on self-care, health awareness, commitment, and mindset shifts that are designed to help leaders Lead well, Look well, Live well, and Love well.

Through this narrative, I hope to empower leaders to make positive changes, demonstrating that navigating and triumphing over these intertwined challenges with faith, determination, and the right strategies is possible. My life is a testament to the resilience of the human spirit and a call to action for leaders to prioritize their health as a cornerstone of their **S.U.C.C.E.S.S.**

The year 2009 started like every other year. Each January 1st, I am excited about new beginnings and new opportunities. The immense feeling of hope, renewal, and a fresh restart fuels me to forgive myself for what I did not do the year before and resolve to do it in the current year.

In February of 2009, my family and I received what we thought was the worst news ever. Our dear mother, Queenie Victoria Thompson, was rushed to the hospital. She had a mild stroke. As we gathered around her bed, she was cognizant and hopeful that she would overcome that setback. As the leader of our family, a single mother of seven grown children and seven grandchildren, she was determined to bounce back after her setback to do what she loved: spending time with her family, singing for the Lord, and cooking our favorite meals. The doctors also encouraged us that she would do just that, and she did.

After two months in the hospital, many tests, rehabilitation, and much love, prayers, and support from her family, her church, and her neighbors, in April 2009, my mother's and my birthday month, our mother was released from the hospital and the rehabilitation center with a clean bill of health and no residual effects of the stroke. God is so good!

After caring for my mother, I gave myself an early birthday gift. You know, ladies, that gift that we give ourselves every year, that yearly appointment that we dread, the one where we are undressed from the bottom down and in stirrups on a cold, hard, padded table, and with a very instructive procedure that leaves us most vulnerable, but it is also the appointment that we know that we must keep. Now that is a power nugget right there - keep all medical appointments, particularly that one, whether sexually active or not.

That appointment turned into another; I was before two gynecologic oncologists before I knew it. Yes, two cancer specialists. With empathy and concern, I heard these words, *"Ms. Jones, you have been diagnosed with stage three Cervical Cancer - Papillary Serous Carcinoma of the cervix. It is high-grade and quite vicious, as you are already in stage 3."* Of course, I was in denial. I had a shock wave go across my body, and then I was back to reality within seconds or minutes. Who knew? I certainly had no clue because I had no symptoms or familial history. BTW- I received this news while on my lunch break from work, as the surgical team contacted me to confirm my surgery for a diagnosis I knew nothing about. I was still waiting for the results of my biopsy.

I could not understand how the ugliness that they claimed was growing viciously inside of me, and that could potentially kill me. How was that possible? My intelligent brain could not comprehend it. There was no precursor for this diagnosis, and let us not forget, I had no symptoms, no irregularities, and no familial history. But was there a precursor?

At the time of my diagnosis, I was every bit of 362 pounds. I looked good, and I felt good. Yes, I looked good because if I did not think and believe it, nobody else would, right? I was divorced one year ago, but I am doing great in my career as a leader with my agency and making great strides in leading successful teams. Nevertheless, I needed more information and a better understanding of the news I received. I did what any intelligent person would do; I began to research and ask a ton of questions. After careful research, I found out those 362 pounds were my warning, my precursor, my danger of cancer.

The Centers for Disease Control (CDC) (https://www.cdc.gov/cancer/risk-factors/obesity.html) has studies that reflect that 40% of the cancers in America are related to obesity. Wow! *Disclaimer:* I am not implying that everyone who is obese will have cancer; what I am saying is that science does reflect that there is a cancer/obesity link. In fact, in recent years, the CDC has highlighted the alarming connection between obesity and cancer. Obesity is not just a condition; it is a significant risk factor for various health issues, including cancer.

The CDC identified nine types of cancer that have a strong correlation with obesity in the United States, and five are listed below:

1. Breast Cancer (Postmenopausal)

2. Colorectal Cancer

3. Esophageal Adenocarcinoma

4. Liver Cancer

5. Ovarian Cancer

Obesity affects the body in many ways. For many, receiving a cancer diagnosis linked to obesity is a wake-up call that necessitates life-changing and transformative decisions.

After consulting with the oncologists, I advised them that I needed some time. The doctors reminded me that because of the viciousness of the cancer that they diagnosed, I did not have time. They advised that if I did not have the surgery within the next few days, but no later than a week, I would certainly die because once the cancer spreads to any major organ, they would not open me up. I insisted that I needed time because I was faced with a storm, and at that moment, I was in duress, and I needed to send out my SOS for healing enforcement.

After both doctors gave me a death sentence, that I would die, I still knew that there was still greatness left in me, and I just could not hear of a death sentence. I left the doctor's office and called on a few key people I knew who knew the words in the worth of prayer. I called Mother Laura Heard. Everyone needs a prayer warrior like Mother Laura Heard in their life. I then called a couple of other prayer warriors, including my now-late ex-husband and my son's father, Anthony Maurice Jones, Sr. Although divorced, we remained great friends and co-parents of our amazing son, Anthony Maurice Jones, II. Because we were still so close when it came to all our son's business. After our separation and divorce, I prayed that God would make me a *"Better Woman"* and not *a "Bitter Woman."* A better woman, I am indeed!

When I told my ex-husband the news, he was kind and compassionate but quite shocked. He said, *"We will get through this as a family, sweetheart."* He immediately stood with me and by me during my entire ordeal.

One of the strategies that helped me was knowing my community of support. You must know those who will stand in faith with you when you are facing a storm. I had to do what I would normally do in any storm. I had to get into a shelter, shut out the storm, and shut into God. I had to not only join my faith with their faith, but I had to believe that I was going to come through that storm because I wanted to live, and there was no way in the world that I was going to accept those death appointments at that time. Sure, my good book (Bible) says it is appointed unto man, once to die, but I did not plan to keep that sentence then.

I faced a couple of other dilemmas; I could not tell our mother what I had just found out. Not right away, anyway. She was still in her recovery and doing amazingly well. I could not imagine sharing the news with her and setting her back by taking the news too badly. Our son was accepted into a very prestigious magnet high school, Cranbrook Kingswood, in Bloomfield Hills, MI, as a boarding student on a full scholarship. He was completing the 9th grade, and his finals were the following week, from my diagnosis. If I shared the news with him before he could complete his finals, I risked the chance of him possibly failing and missing out on the fully paid scholarship to attend this school. I could not take that risk. His education meant the world to his daddy and me. Here I was, facing life or death, and I was still putting others before me. I had to in this instance. I am glad that I did. The timing was everything, and I would not change how I planned to share the news with everyone.

The fight to live was on. I had to choose life and living. This was personal. Facing a cancer diagnosis can be overwhelming, but it can also be a powerful catalyst for change. In my case, choosing life meant embarking on a journey of transformation and a true test and testament of my faith. Each day presented a new challenge and opportunity to make decisions that would positively impact my health and well-being. As a leader, the stress and demands of daily decisions can be immense, often pushing us to the brink of burnout. It is crucial to remember that Leaders' Lives Matter Too.

Leadership comes with its own set of challenges and responsibilities. The constant demands on our time, talent, and resources can leave us feeling drained and overwhelmed, yet empowering and rewarding. However, amidst these pressures, it is essential to prioritize our own health and well-being. As leaders, we often place the needs of others above our own, but self-care is not selfish; it is necessary.

After three days of fasting, praying, and lying before the Lord, on the third day, I heard these words, *"You shall live and not die, and this will never return again. And, I have called you into the ministry."*

Hallelujah! I began giving God all the glory, honor, and praise that He deserved. I also knew that it was time to shift my mindset to begin living my life on the other side of the diagnosis. Although I respected the doctors for their diagnosis, I fully TRUSTED God for my prognosis. I knew where to draw the line of my faith with the medical team because I needed the assistance of my Chief Physician, my Lord and Savior, Jesus Christ. Of course, God could have miraculously healed me; however, He had chosen another path for me.

On June 29, 2009, I had surgery to remove the cancer. By the way, the doctors were shocked that I was still alive and that the cancer had not spread any further. It was a first for them. Remember, they told me that if I did not have the surgery within a few days or at least a week or so, they would not perform the surgery because of the type of aggressive cancer and that it would have spread to my major organs. If it did spread, it would be unnecessary to open me up because it would be too late. Well, they said that in mid-May. I remind you that the surgery was on June 29, 2009. Look at God! Not only did I surpass the few days to one week or so requirement for surgery, I waited an entire month and a half. God knew what He was doing so that, medically and physically, no one could take credit for what He was doing in and through me.

In 2011, when I reached a turning point, March 23, 2011, became the absolutely worst day of my life and that of my family. Our dear mother made her transition from earth to glory. It was not expected. I was the last person with her the night before. Rest on in glory, dear mother. We love you.

Despite surviving cancer, I was still struggling with obesity, the very condition that had contributed to my illness. I realized that I needed to make a drastic change if I wanted to lead effectively and live a fulfilling life. This decision led to a quest for permanent weight release, not weight loss, but weight release, because whatever is lost can potentially be found. I had no intention of ever finding those pounds again. I have successfully released over 200 pounds, and I am more committed than ever to maintaining my health.

Through my journey, I developed **The Seven S.U.C.C.E.S.S. Strategies for Transformation** that were crucial to my journey. These strategies can help anyone seeking to improve their health and well-being:

1. Self-care is Not Weak or Selfish; It is Necessary!

- As leaders, our lives matter, too. Taking time for self-care yields the greatest return on investment. You are worth the effort and attention.

2. Understand the Importance of Your Health Numbers!

- Understand and know your numbers and other vital statistics. Awareness is crucial because what you do not know can harm you. For instance, hypertension rates are disproportionately high among African Americans, underscoring the importance of regular health check-ups.
    - How much do you weigh/date? _______/_______
    - What is your blood pressure/date? _______/_______
    - What is your cholesterol level/date? _______/_______
    - What is your blood sugar level/date? _______/_______
    - What is your blood type/date? _______/_______

3. Cultivate a Community of Authentic Relationships!

- Building genuine relationships can empower both others and yourself. Remember, your well-being is as important as that of those you lead and love.

4. Champion Your Own Cause and Commit to Self-Check-Ins!

- Strive to be the person you look up to. Show others that it is possible to prioritize self-care while leading effectively. Your team is always watching you and taking notice. What a beautiful opportunity to model leadership than starting with leading yourself first. People began to champion and encourage me more as they saw me take the lead in my health and wellness journey, and many began doing the same.

- Schedule regular check-ins with yourself, just as you would with your team. Use these moments to assess your health, set goals, and plan for your well-being.

- Be relentless about advocating for your health. You are a partner in your health care.

5. Elevate Your Value and Your Expectations!

- When you expect that there is more for you, you nurture it, walk in it, and feed it until you are hungry for more. DO NOT waste time.

- Walk in your greatness and put the world on notice that you are still here, present, and accounted for. Will it be easy? No! But there is no greater joy than leading by the Power of your Example and not by the Example of your Power.

6. Share and Get Excited About Your Transformation!

- Share your journey with those you love. Your enthusiasm and commitment to self-improvement can inspire and benefit others.

7. Shift Your Mindset and Start Today!

- A **Shift** or a slight change in perspective can make all the difference. Embrace shifts in your journey and confront the issues weighing you down. Taking care of yourself is about prioritizing your own needs and well-being. You deserve to be at your best.

- Start now! Make today your January 1st!

In his book "**Make Today Count,**" John Maxwell emphasizes the importance of daily discipline for success. Reflecting on the decisions we make concerning our health, it's vital to identify and practice the necessary disciplines every day.

The journey from Cancer to Comeback, along with fighting obesity to health, is possible. By adopting these **Seven S.U.C.C.E.S.S. Strategies** and making a daily commitment to our well-being, we can transform our lives as we lead by example. Remember, Leaders' Lives Matter Too. **Leader, you matter!** Prioritizing our health is not just a personal victory; it's an essential part of effective leadership to Lead well, Look well, Live well, and Love well.

DR. LISA YVETTE JONES

Chief Caring Officer(CCO) and Leadership Coach

Dr. Lisa Yvette Jones, the Chief Caring Officer and Leadership Coach of iC.A.R.E. Leadership LLC. She empowers professional women to cultivate authentic relationships, elevate performance, and create human-centered workplaces. She inspires leaders to prioritize self-care while caring for others, transforming the employee experience with compassion, competence, and excellent execution.

Having decades of experience in leadership development, training, coaching, mentoring, and counseling, she has built a meritorious acumen in influencing career professionals to prioritize their health and their love for self-care.

Dr. Lisa Yvette Jones holds a Bachelor of Arts degree in Business Administration, a Master of Arts degree in Counseling, and an Honorary Doctor of Philosophy in Business Administration.

Connect with Dr. Jisa

www.LisaYvetteJones.com

LisaYvetteJonesCoaching@gmail.com

1(248) 397-5227

THE STORY OF TRAVIS ANDREWS

MOVING THROUGH TRAUMA TO PURPOSE

The First Fracture

I was 9 when it happened.

The significant emotional event that shaped life and the decisions I made. Until I refused to stay numb and self-destruct. The day felt normal til I didn't.

That afternoon, I was told that my Nan had died. I loved Nan so much; my favourite memories were making fake flowers with her for weddings. They were made out of stockings and wire coat hangers back then. Nan was the calm in the chaos. I do not remember where I was when I was told, but I do remember being in my room that evening, sobbing quietly. It was a soft, confused cry of a 9-year-old child who did not understand death or what this would mean for my life and my family. But I did know something really sad had happened.

As I sobbed, my mum came into my room. She was crying too, a soft, gentle, sad cry. Mum was really devastated, as I am sure you could imagine. (She had just lost her mum to a long battle with cancer.) Then mum said something that would define the course of my life. Something that, completely unintentionally, would send me down a pathway that would shape my life for the next 28 years, and draw me to the edge of a dark, deep void.

Mum bargained that if I stopped crying, she would also stop. That was the deal, no explanation in the delivery, just a condition. My emotions controlled hers. This, I assume, would allow her to cope with her own sadness by easing mine.

I did not have the language or understanding for it at the time, but the instruction resonated deeply. If I stopped, mum stopped. The room went deathly quiet, as did the noise within me. This memory is strangely clear amidst a life where very few memories are. Not because of the grief, but because it was the first time something had shut off permanently deep within me.

Understanding death in its fullest at the time was impossible. This was my first experience of death. But what my body did understand was that if I expressed emotion, Mum cried and/or felt pain. I stopped expressing, and Mum stopped crying.

It was simple math for my body back then: realising that feeling something and expressing that emotion could cause harm to another. So, the crying ended, and with it the cause.

From that point on, my emotions became a threat. Not only to me, but also to the people around me. If my sadness could make my mum cry, what else could it do? The safest thing my mind understood to do at the time was to abandon that part of me; Not acknowledge it, not feel through it, nor process it. But abandon it.

This was such a significant experience; there was no dramatic internal experience, just my body's quiet response, to disconnect and be strong for my mum. There was no time to grieve, no time to understand, no time to process, no time to say goodbye. Just bury it all, don't feel, don't acknowledge, and therefore, don't harm.

Grief, sadness, loss, hurt, and pain. Cause and effect. These words and concepts came a lot later. Back then, it was simple maths for the body with an underdeveloped mind. To disconnect and protect—one input, one output. Disconnect the input.

What makes this memory stand out is not the emotion; I don't remember what I felt about my Nan dying, although I was left feeling I did not get to say goodbye correctly. I do remember, though, that something deep within me had shifted. And I remember the stillness that followed. Everything else from around that age is vague, or missing from my memory, as are other massive chunks of my childhood. Time frames and dates are only estimates to the best of my knowledge. Not entirely accurate. But strangely, that moment is very vivid. Not because it hurt, but because it taught me not to hurt.

What I did not understand at the time, though, was that I had left a massive piece of me behind, because I could still sense other people's emotional states. I mean, they affected me greatly. I just stopped generating my own. I did not respond with feeling. Other people's pain was easier to detect than my own.

Becoming The Mask

From that day on, I didn't just stop crying; I stopped being the source of any emotional disruption. I did not know it then, but I did start learning to live through everyone else. If the people around me were happy, I would feel a bit of that, too. But when things went quiet, when there was no talking, no laughter, no noise or activity, that's when it got hard. Silence wasn't peace for me; it was overwhelming. It was my thoughts getting louder, and I hated being left alone with them.

I never felt confident in myself. I never felt like I was enough. This constant feeling that something was always missing, as if I were the only one who did not have what everyone else seemed to have. So, I found comfort among the people I hung out with, most of whom were considered the *"Bad Group"*. They were the tough ones. The ones that nobody messed with. On the outside, that made me look strong; on the inside, I was anything but. I think I felt safer being around them because they had what I didn't, presence. They did not have to explain who they were; they just were.

Reflecting, all these years later, I find it unusual that I never had to stand up for myself. Others have always done that for me, and I am still not sure why. Perhaps they saw or sensed something in me that I couldn't see in myself. Maybe I gave off the strong impression that I needed protecting, without even realising it. However, the truth was that I was intimidated most of the time, especially at school or in social settings. It was the total opposite of what I knew at home.

My home was filled with love, too much love at times. There was no room for anger or for rough edges, perhaps a consequence of my dad being forbidden to raise his voice or his hands to us. If my brothers and I argued with one another, we were told to go down to the park and sort it out among ourselves. Mum could no longer stand aggression. But we never did, as we were always shut down by Mum before we got that aggressive with each other, as Mum was very protective of us, which I now understand all too clearly.

From an early age, Mum was subjected to a childhood of violence, abuse, and fear, beginning with her own Mother (Nan) being beaten by her Dad (Pop). (Pop used to sit mum, her brothers, and sisters down so they could watch Nan get beaten) This cruel regime then extended to her and her brothers and sisters, and then the abuse extended beyond their household, as my mum and others were sexually abused by their neighbour. Consequently, protecting us and providing stability and safety was paramount to her. So for mum, protecting us meant keeping the world as soft as possible.

The problem with such well-intentioned protection, though, was that the world – particularly where I lived – was anything but safe, secure, or soft. And so, I wasn't prepared for it. I learned early that at home, emotions caused pain, and outside, emotions equalled weakness. And weakness in that harsh world meant suffering and misery. So, my mask became my protection, my way of staying somewhere in between; safe, likable, and untouchable. Perhaps my saviour was my ability to make people laugh, read a room, blend into the environment, so I never revealed what was going on beneath the surface.

As I grew older, that mask remained firmly in place to the point that I was unaware that I was wearing it. This was now my identity, regardless of who I let into my life, including friends, partners, and anyone I connected with. I started attracting people who had the same missing parts as me, sometimes even more so than I did. It's challenging looking back at who I had become, but it just made sense at the time. Broken people and pieces often recognise each other and are drawn together.

The friendships and relationships I built back then were far from healthy. They were built on a flawed foundation of what was missing, not what was whole. So, I was drawn to people who were the opposite of me: unpredictable, emotional, or unstable. Unconsciously, this was my desperate attempt to become whole. But I had no idea that all I was succeeding in doing was befriending people who were more broken than I was and who would lead me, or I would follow willingly, into a darker world. This was the spiral that, unbeknownst to me at the time, would descend to potentially life-threatening places. Foolishly, I thought I was being loyal, caring, or protective. However, I was really stuck in a cycle, trying to fix others when I could not fix myself.

Hanging around with these people became my normal. The more toxic they got, the more I tried to hold them together; I did not feel the emotion or pain of it. Nor could I see the endless hurt all around me. Day after day, I just kept showing up, doing what I thought was right. I thought love meant staying at a distance, and that loyalty meant never walking away. But the truth is, if you do not know what hurt is, you cannot understand what love is either. And at the time, I knew neither. I was numb, stumbling from one dark day to the next.

So, I kept going, doing my utmost to cling to the false sense of belonging, trying to hold everything together. I didn't feel hurt; I just felt tired and numb, confused about why things never seemed to change, yet unable to imagine another way of being.

The Domestic Relationship - The Cost of Staying Numb

The numbness didn't just stay locked inside of me; it came with me everywhere I went. It shaped how I connected with people, what I tolerated, and what I called love. I kept finding myself in situations that mirrored the same quiet disconnection I had learned as a kid.

The pattern that had previously shaped both my existence and my relationships with those around me continued. In 2008, I found myself 2 years into a personal relationship that was founded on two people, not just me this time, once again trying to fill the void within myself. I was oblivious to the flawed and toxic foundation on which our relationship was based.

We both escaped the world that troubled us so much through the consumption of alcohol and cannabis, trying to quiet what we did not know how to face. I drank a lot back then, and she smoked a lot of weed.

The first time my partner hit me, it started over something as insignificant and ridiculous as dishwashing liquid. I had used too much liquid, and there were too many bubbles on the dishes after washing. This memory is as clear as day, as though it were yesterday. After a few drinks, I wasn't thinking much. Then, quite suddenly, out of nowhere, she wacked me; it was a beauty. She cracked me square in the nose. For a few moments, I stood in complete shock, struggling to comprehend the stinging, jarring blow. But it was not the pain that shocked me; it was the silence in me that ensued.

Nothing moved. Not my body, not my voice, not my emotions, just complete stillness. For what seemed like an eternity, I froze. I didn't hit back. I didn't even raise my voice. My only reaction was to hold her up against the wall and say quietly, *"If you ever hit me again, this is what will happen"*, and I hit the wall next to her head; Not to scare her, but to show her something I did not understand myself.

And of course, consistent with my luck back then, I struck one of the beams in the wall and shattered my hand completely. Again, there was no pain, though, at that time, as it was masked by my drunken state and my usual state of numbness.

The next morning was different, though. The pain was there— broken bones, surgery, two pins, and eight weeks in a removable cast with intense physio. This incident not only had an impact on me personally at the time. It impacted everyone in my existence who cared about me. It affected my parents and 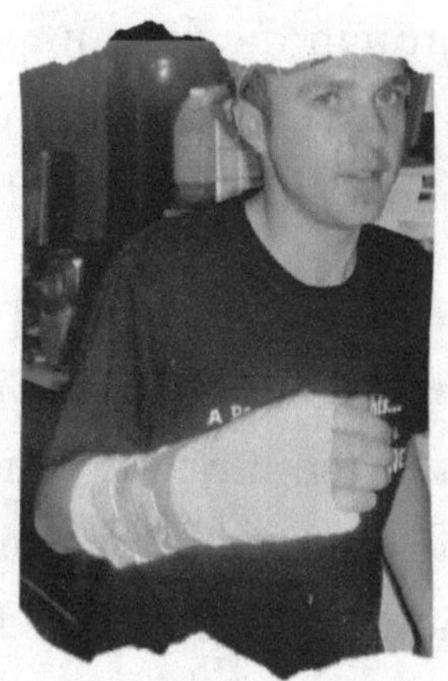 others, as I could not drive and needed a lift to and from work and to physio. It impacted my career at the time. I was very lucky. I was a highly valued employee and was given an admin role until my hand recovered. I was a heavy vehicle mechanic at the time, working on heavy machinery, and could not complete the work. I was very lucky to still be employed.

Of course, I recognise now that I should have walked away right then, but back in those dark days and years, I didn't walk away from pain; I adapted to it, as I had when my nan died.

12 weeks later, it happened again. This was the day that my life nearly ended. I'd been working on arranging for my partner's brother to start a job with me, and soon after he started, we finished work early one day after attending an electrical short course for the buses we were working on at the time.

I said to him, *"Let's get a case of beer and mow the lawns, so then I will not have to do them on the weekend"*. As usual, I was restless and couldn't stand still. What I needed was a distraction to quiet the noise in my mind. Well, I did not only get a case of beer. I also got a bottle of spirits and was having straight shots with each fresh beer.

By the time we had finished, I was half cut, no cigarettes left, and feeling the kind of peace that only comes from being comfortably numb from alcohol. My partner had been asleep inside all day. It was approximately 3 pm, she woke up cranky, fuelled by the absence of weed, smokes, and money, already fired up. Now, inside the house, the second she realised my cigarettes were gone, she completely lost it, accusing me of giving hers to her brother for helping me mow the lawn, leaving her with none and no money to buy more.

In a crazy rage, she yelled abuse at me, telling me I could have been doing something quieter while she was sleeping. Before I had any chance to process what was happening, she had cracked me again, square in the nose, but much harder this time. Instantly, blood spattered and flowed everywhere around me, gushing from my now broken nose. It was not like the first time, she had busted me up; it was messy. Again, I did not react; I just walked calmly outside, bleeding the most unnatural way. Her brother assumed I had headbutted the wall, so he just stayed out of it.

She was inside the house, stalking me from window to window as I stood outside, screaming abuse at me through the glass. To release whatever I was experiencing, I punched the fibro sheeted wall a few times as I moved down the side of the house. She kept following and yelling abuse at me from window to window. By the time I reached the kitchen side, the last side of the house, I'd had enough. With one final act of frustration and rage, I punched through the glass of the window as I reached in to grab her.

That's when I saw it, the blood squirting and pumping out of my arm with every heartbeat. I'd severed the main artery in two places; I now had blood all over my face, and now gushing and pumping from my arm. I was a bloody mess. My life was running out of me before my very eyes.

She called the police, not the ambulance, and told them I was smashing up the house. What she didn't mention was that she had assaulted me and busted me up.

Shortly after, the police arrived with no care as to the seriousness of my condition, assuming I was the aggressor and that my injuries were self-inflicted. All they were worried about was if I had aids or diseases as they prepared to arrest me without calling for an ambulance. I have no doubt those officers would of watched me die that day.

If it were not for my neighbour arriving home at that same time, I have no doubt I would have died and would not be sharing this story with you today. He saw me and immediately ran inside to grab a towel and his phone. Hurriedly, he wrapped the towel around my arm and sat on my arm on the sidewalk while he called the ambulance. There was a significant delay in the ambulance being called; its arrival was well overdue, during which my parents and brother were called. Consequently, they arrive at the scene before the ambulance. By the time the paramedics had arrived, I was going into shock. I remember saying I felt like I was going to shit myself and said, *"Can I go to the toilet?"*

One of the paramedics said to me. *"Mate, you're going into shock if you need to shit 'SHIT', we are getting you to the hospital, we have to go."*

Next thing I knew, I was fading away. As the ambulance raced towards the hospital, the only vague awareness I had was the jolt from the road obstacles, which I guess was the concrete median strip dividing the lanes. Then, nothing. I was gone. That day, I had my neighbour, then the wonderful paramedics, to thank for saving my life.

By the time the ambulance arrived at Nepean Hospital, I had bled out, and my body had tapped out. I was announced unresponsive on arrival to hospital. Something much more substantial and profound had taken hold of me that day. I had no blood left to bleed out, but the ICU team had blood reserves waiting for me in the emergency room.

And here's the thing: I survived, but I didn't feel like I had survived. I wasn't angry, or scared, or grateful. I just felt nothing. Just the same cold, calm that has been with me since I was 9. The cost of staying numb.

Looking back, it took me almost a decade to reflect on that experience and turn it around. I always blamed my ex-fiancé, believing that if she had not hit me, if she had not aggravated me, none of that would have happened. The truth is, looking back and searching my heart, that day was not about her or what she did; It was about me. It was about the pattern of survival. It was about the need to protect everyone else but myself. It was about fixing and staying numb. There were ample chances to walk away from the relationship after the first assault, and many after the 2nd I could vacate the property straight after being hit. But I didn't. You see, numbness keeps you where you do not belong. It tells you that staying calm means you're in control. It tells you chaos is normal. And that is the danger, though, because when you cannot feel pain, you also can not feel fear. And without fear, you stop recognising when you're in danger, even when it's your own life on the line.

That day was not my turning point. It was just another layer of numbness burying what I was still not ready to face.

Aftermath: The Years That Followed

After that, I should have changed everything. But the truth is, I didn't.

That day, I was somehow blessed to walk out of the hospital with my right arm still attached to my body. There was delay after delay getting me into surgery due to other emergencies continuing to roll in. There was even discussion of removing my arm as it was going gangrene. Heavily stitched up, bandaged, and in another cast, all holding me together, I walked away, but inside, nothing was repaired.

The numbness still engulfed me.

I was not angry, I was not sad, I was just flat, like life had pushed pause and forgot to hit play again. I knew something very bad had happened, but I did not feel that thought. I told myself I had had enough of the chaos, but I didn't change the pattern. I just changed the faces.

Not long after, I drifted into another relationship, which had moments of calm and even a sense of hope. My new partner had 2 boys from a previous relationship, and I wanted to be something steady for them. I thought maybe if I could be that man for her and for them, then I'd finally be that man for me.

Sadly, though, we were both lost. We are both still carrying our own pain and confusion, just hiding it better. She had her history, and I had mine, that neither of us could outrun. Instead of building something stable, we built something on top of a plethora of old wounds.

Don't get me wrong, there was love in our relationship, I can't deny that, but it was love tangled up in fear and insecurity, and I could not feel or express it. Again, the pattern engulfed us, as drugs and alcohol played their part. Like a silent, simple switch, turn off the thoughts that never stopped talking.

We were blessed, at least, when our beautiful daughter, Jessie, came into our lives. Jessie was the one thing that felt pure, untouched by the chaos. Holding Jessie, I vividly remember thinking, maybe this is finally my chance to do things differently. To find myself. To fight for a purpose so much bigger than who I was.

But when you haven't healed, you end up repeating. The same numbness that protected me as a kid became the same numbness that stopped me from being fully present as a father. I could provide, I could protect, and I was always there unconditionally. But feeling, really feeling, giving all of myself was still something I didn't know how to do.

Our relationship eventually broke down. It wasn't explosive like the last one. It just quietly dissolved. Two people trying to find themselves but losing each other in the process because neither of us could mend ourselves, or each other. The holes inside were just too big. The one thing that did stay pure and untouched was our daughter and the roles we each played as parents in Jessie's life. I mean, it has not gone without great struggle at times, having different opinions, standards, beliefs, and values. But we have always found a middle ground without going legal and entering a courtroom. We have always respected each other's roles in Jessie's life and never let our differences, views, or opinions have an impact on that. We have always had equal shared care and always will. I stayed in this relationship a lot longer than I should of. As I was concerned for the boys going through a second failed relationship, and I was concerned about my role changing in Jessie's life. I had all these stories playing out in my head, and what I experienced was the complete opposite.

When it finally ended, I wasn't heartbroken. I was hollow. There's a big difference, but once again, I still didn't see how the pattern ran through it all. The numbness, the need to protect, the habit of fixing everyone but me.

For years after that, I kept surrounding myself with the same type of energy, unpredictable people, toxic friendships, and unstable dark environments. It's funny how the body finds familiarity even in dysfunction, because dysfunction becomes your comfortable place. I told myself repeatedly, this is just the type of people I connect with and get along with. But really, I was clinging to the noise, to the chaos, so I wouldn't have to face the silence within me. These people were a direct reflection of the disconnect and numbness within me.

I could feel myself gradually changing, though. Sadly, not for the better. There was a point at which I realised that if I continued living this way, I would become a combination of all the toxicity around me, the people, places, and dark environments where all bad things existed. And that scared me, not because I was afraid to die, but because I knew I was already disappearing and did not have the strength or courage to fight back.

I was at a crossroads, the point in my life where if I did not take a different route, then the one I had been trapped on for so many years would run out, and I would disappear over the edge. This road was one-way, with no return. There was no turning back.

It was not a massive awakening or a miracle moment; it was simple, fleeting, and just a glimpse of light. But it was enough, though, for me to take a look at myself in the mirror with honesty. I knew full well that I could be doing a lot better than I was.

The Turning Point

For a long time, I knew I wanted to change. But I had no idea where to even begin. Reaching out for help, or even knowing what to say, was so far beyond my capabilities. I couldn't see another path forward. I couldn't visualise it, and I couldn't feel it. All I knew was that I did not want to go the route of mainstream health or traditional therapy. I'd tried numbing, avoiding, and pretending, and none of it had worked for me.

It began with something small, a simple action.

I started to Google to see if people had come back from the same or similar self-destructive patterns and behaviours that I had lived with for so long. In particular, I was searching for men who had turned around their numbness and inability to feel; People who started over after losing everything.

I wasn't looking for advice; I was looking for proof. Proof that it was possible for someone like me. To my surprise, what I found in a short time was powerful. I read story after story about people who had come back from the same kind of self-destruction that I was living through. People who had survived tragedy, loss, and pain far beyond what I could imagine, but still managed to rise again. When Jessie came into the world, the math changed. I wasn't solving for survival anymore. I was solving for her. She turned a vague wish to change into a reason I couldn't ignore.

Their stories did not make my journey any less heavy, but they made it possible. For the first time, I saw a glimpse of something different. A life that wasn't ruled by chaos, numbness, and drifting aimlessly. A life that might mean something.

And that is where it all began, not with a big breakthrough, but with a realisation that if it was possible for others, then maybe, just maybe, it was possible for me too.

Jessie became the mirror I could not look away from anymore.

The Awakening

The belief turned into action fast. Within weeks, life and the universe started lining things up for me. Like it knew I was finally ready. My brother, at the time, was a director and partner in a mid-sized construction company. Approximately five people were working in the office at the time, all heavy smokers, and all had just decided to quit smoking together.

They had decided to give a hypnotherapist who offered a one-session guarantee, a go. It was $500. Expensive to some but cheap compared to a pack-a-day habit in Australia.

Remarkably, they all quit smoking at that first session. When my brother told me, I didn't hesitate and said, "Who is she? Where is she? And what's her number?" If it worked for them, why would it not work for me?

I wasn't going for help to stop smoking (although I was still smoking at the time), but my motivation was to quit my heavy meth addiction. Deep down, I knew the addiction was not the root; it was the Mask. The excuse. The easiest way to justify what I was or was not feeling. It was just another way to stay numb.

So, I booked a consultation.

And this remarkable woman, this therapist, a master of her craft, rocked my world. The moment I met her, I felt an overwhelming sense of calm, like I had never felt before. Safe. Seen. Her presence alone softened something within me. I opened up completely and let out my pain of not being able to change, my shame, and my desire to change my life. I told her everything. Perhaps for the first time in my life, I felt truly heard. Not once did she make me feel judged, wrong, or broken.

After 30 minutes, she looked at me and said something that didn't make sense at first.

"The last thing you need to focus on is your addiction. Focus on the rest, and your addiction will sort itself out."

Part of me thought she was crazy. But another part, the deeper part, trusted her completely. We agreed on a six-week program consisting of six sessions of guided hypnosis. What unfolded in those six sessions changed everything. Everything!

Each session peeled back layer after layer, opening a door I had no idea existed. There were moments so intense, so far beyond logic, that, to this day, I can't comprehend or adequately explain. It stirred emotions I had never felt or known existed. It was so spiritual, so profound that, in moments, I felt reborn, as though I suddenly connected with everything that I had never felt.

I had my first spiritual experiences there. Moments that rattled me so profoundly, I did not make it to the sixth session. I was not ready to sit in that space and fully face myself yet. But the transformation had already started. It was like life itself had begun clearing space. Friends and old environments started falling away without any effort. My old identity, the mask I had worn, that was fused to my face for decades, began to crack apart. And, finally, I could see a light through that crack that had alluded me since I was a young child.

After one of the sessions, I stopped by the pub on the way home for a slap on the pokies. That day I lost many, but, ironically, I also blissfully lost my phone. Because of it, a lot of my contacts from that dark, toxic world that I had existed in for so long were gone.

Shortly after that, my Facebook account was hacked, leaving me unable to verify enough information to retrieve it. Now, everyone from my old world had vanished. It was as if the universe were erasing my past for me. All those people, places, and things were disappearing. Finally, that new pathway was starting to unfold, and I now needed to find the courage to stay on it. And not go chasing down old contacts.

That's when something deep shifted. My eyes were now open, for the first time in 28 years, and I could finally start to see and feel new ways forward. But patterns don't disappear that easily. That same old cycle, to numb, to protect, and fix others, came back, just in a different form.

This time, it surfaced out of curiosity. I wanted to understand what had just happened to me, what I had experienced in hypnosis, so I could help others experience the same. So, I signed up for a Fast Track hypnosis course, which introduced me to NLP and Timeline Therapy. All of it helped me understand my past and the inner mechanics of my mind. However, it also helped me avoid my feelings in a more intelligent way.

Outsmarting my own pain instead of healing it. It took time and humility to see the pattern clearly. But once I did, I started breaking down those loops. Breaking down the overthinking, severe stress, and anxiety, and the constant need to fix. Slowly, I started to win the only battle that ever mattered: The one between me and my own mind.

Because that's where our default settings are. Where everything begins and ends. Inside.

The Continuation

Change can happen overnight. But transformation, the kind that lasts, takes work. Constant, conscious work. What happened in that chair during hypnosis was the spark. What's happened since then has been the fire, the daily choice to keep showing up no matter how I feel, to keep digging deeper, to keep turning towards what's real instead of what's easy.

When I started to see how I had shifted, I felt called to help others do the same. I began coaching people from all walks of life, including men and women of diverse ages, backgrounds, and struggles. And what I realised was this: The patterns I carried for so long weren't just mine.

They show up everywhere, in our professional lives, our personal lives, our relationships, our workplaces, our friendships. They hide behind achievement, perfection, people pleasing, addiction, and staying numb. Different mask, same roots. And when people felt safe enough to take off their masks, that's where the transformation happened.

Most of my Coaching sessions became honest, raw conversations. People want to be heard. Many had not felt safe enough to express what they truly felt. They'd carried years, or several decades, of stored tension, emotion, and energy with no outlet. And when they let it out, the relief, the release, the power, it was life-changing. I watched people heal lifelong patterns just by having the space to be seen. To feel safe in their truth. To let their emotions exist without shame or judgment.

Some of these people invested thousands in these sessions. But what they really invested in was themselves, the chance to feel lighter, freer, and stand in their truth. And by holding space for others, I found a deeper connection within myself.

Each session mirrored a part of my own journey back to what I'd first touched in those hypnosis sessions. That higher, quieter part of me that always knew there was more.

From there, I dove deeper into breathwork, embodiment, mind-body-soul connection. I learned to catch thoughts as they formed and redirect them into something meaningful. I started to understand my nervous system, how my body speaks before my mind does, how calm is not a thought. It's a state you learn to hold.

A harsh lesson I learnt was that the people who once seemed like they didn't want to help me did. They just didn't want to waste their time watching me waste mine. You can try everything to help someone, but there will be no meaningful change until they find the inner strength to want to change. When I finally started putting effort into myself, others did too, and they were the ones who cared the most and wanted to help

"Because that's the truth of transformation, the world meets you at the level you meet yourself."

From Survival to Meaning

There is a quiet truth I've come to understand after walking through darkness and finding my way back into the light: trauma does not ask permission before it enters your life — but purpose always waits for an invitation.

For years, I believed my story was one of damage beyond repair. That's what had happened to me. That numbness was strength, silence was safety, and survival was enough. But survival is not living. It is merely staying above water without ever learning how to feel the ocean.

The greatest revelation of my life was not in the pain — it was in discovering that pain does not have the final word. The past is not a prison unless you refuse to walk out of it. That healing doesn't erase the story… it rewrites the ending.

What broke me became the birthplace of what saved me.

The numbness that once protected me eventually became the very thing that suffocated me. And only when I was willing to feel again — really feel — did I finally begin to live. Not perfectly. Not cleanly. But honestly.

Purpose did not arrive as a lightning bolt.

It arrived as a whisper.

A quiet knowing.

A fragile hope.

A single question: *What if your life is not over?*

And from that moment on, change stopped being something I wished for — and became something I chose.

I now understand that our deepest wounds often become our greatest teachers. That the very thing you are trying to outrun may be the doorway into who you were always meant to become. And that which nearly destroyed you may one day become the reason you survive.

This chapter is not about pain.

It is about what pain can become.

It is about the moment you stop running from your past…

and start listening to it.

It is about trading numbness for truth.

Fear for feeling.

Survival for meaning.

It is about accepting this:

You were never weak.

You were wounded.

And wounded things can heal.

"I cracked open because of life.

But I rebuilt myself because of Jessie.

Not because she saved me — but because she deserved a father she'd never have to recover from."

TRAVIS ANDREWS

Transformation Integration Mentor

Breath-work Facilitator

Travis Andrews is a father and transformational advocate dedicated to breaking generational patterns through awareness and conscious growth. After overcoming two decades of addiction, self-destruction, and self-abuse, he committed his life to self-responsibility and understanding how language shapes identity. In his chapter of Stories of Miraculous Transformation, Travis shares an honest reflection on parenting and the unseen impact of words. His message is clear: transformation begins with awareness, not perfection — and he invites others to reconnect, integrate their experiences, and consciously rewrite the patterns they carry forward.

Connect with Travis

Email: travisandrews011@gmail.com

Ph: 0410125087

Facebook: @Travis Andrews

Instagram: @travis1andrews

THE STORY OF PETER SPEZIALE

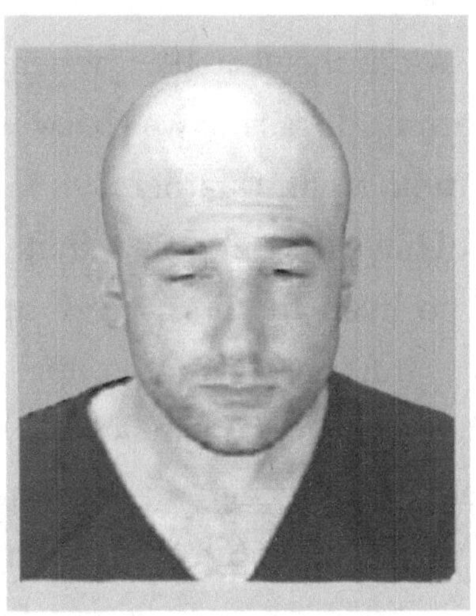

OM MANI PADME HUM

The Jewel Within the Lotus

As I sit here writing this, telling my story for a book about transforming one's life, I cannot help but be in awe. It is a very surreal feeling and seems as if I am lost in a dream. Two and a half decades I spent in perpetual darkness and ignorance of what life could truly be if we just open ourselves up to it. At no point did I believe my life would change from the cycle of addiction, narcotics distribution, prison, rinse and repeat, but here I am with what people consider *"quite a story to tell,"* but to me it is just the amazingly miraculous, wonderful, and sometimes God-awful thing we call *life*.

It starts way back in the year 1981, when I was born into a very wonderful family. I was the wee baby with 3 much older siblings and a mother and father who loved me. My upbringing did not have the things in it that you would expect from someone who lived the life I grew up leading. There was no abuse or trauma. My mother never used foul language and believed if someone hits you, you give them the other cheek. Every night we ate dinner together at the table at 6 pm, and the television had to be turned off. If you were late, you were grounded. This was very important to my mother and still is to this day.

At the age of 7, things took a major turn for all of us when my father was diagnosed with cancer of the esophagus. My father was disintegrating in front of us, and in November, when I was 8, he lost his battle with cancer. The holidays were never quite the same after that. This left my mother raising 4 of us with a part-time job, and she was denied assistance because she owned her home. I can vividly remember my mother openly expressing her grief for about 2 weeks, and then it seemed life simply went on. Now looking back and after being in love myself, I realized what it must have been like for her every night when she closed her bedroom door and lay down alone in her bed, she once shared with my dad. This crash course in death taught us you grieve those who pass, but you must continue with life. The loss of my father made my mother decide to move me from public school (where I was a nerdy white kid) to Catholic school, where I was looked at as the kid who survived public school, and I was happy to run with that persona.

When I was 10, I went with my mother to my grandmother's house. My mother was telling her she did not know what to do about money. Grandma suggested going across the street to talk to her neighbor, who was in the same HVAC trade my father was, and see if he would buy some of the tools my dad had left behind. When talking to him about the situation, he informed her that he had also lost his spouse to cancer. They began going to dinner once a week to talk about their grief, and 2 years later, my mom remarried. Even at 12, I knew I could not argue with the fact that they were destined to meet. This man took on 4 children, 3 of whom were teenagers, and one who was at the beginning of a lifetime of bad decisions, and yet he never once treated us as anything other than his own children. He deserves a Purple Heart for that, and they are still together to this day.

At this point, I am entering 6th grade, and this is where it all began to go wrong. I began using marijuana from time to time, and the one thing that caught my attention was that for us to have it, someone somewhere was making money by selling it. So, in the 7th grade, I began to save up my allowance to buy enough to make some money. I will never forget my first transaction in the drug world. A friend had moved to a different neighborhood and knew some older teens who were going to a hotel party and wanted to spend $50 on weed. I got a ride to his house, and when we got there, we found ourselves in a room with just us and 5 or 6 of them. They proceeded to hand me $10 and told us to get out or get our asses kicked. We graciously said goodbye and left quickly. If only that had changed my course. By the end of 8th grade, I had more money than one needs at 14, spent bathroom breaks shooting dice, lost my virginity, and was experimenting with pain pills, Xanax, and drinking. I won't lie; I was having the time of my life.

When it was time for high school, I decided to attend a different Catholic High School than the one most of my friends were going to, and I am not quite sure why I made that choice. Cathedral High School was where the wealthier kids from Indianapolis's north side went. I did not fit in at all, but that was ok, because I didn't need to be their friend to sell them weed, and business there was damn good. One day, while shooting dice with one of my regular opponents, he asked if I could sell crack like I do weed. I knew what crack was, but that was the extent of it. I didn't know anyone who did it, but I told him that if it can be sold, I can sell it. He proceeded to hand me a big bag of $20 rocks, told me how to price it, how much I owed him, and told me to let him know when I needed more. Simple as that, at the age of 14, I became a crack dealer. At least that was the plan. I had no idea who to sell it to, so I spread the word. I'll be damned, it turned out many people of all ages were messing with it. White, black, old, young, poor, or from wealthy families. Crack made its way into every place like water through a creek bed, and these customers were not the mellow kind I was used to. This went on for over a year, having tons of money and partying with friends, paying no attention to the addictions I was forming. To my teenage mind, life could not be better.

One of my customers was the stepdad of a friend of mine. My friend told him I had some, and he began by getting a $20 rock, and then another and another and another until I had to leave for dinner at six o'clock. He knew that was the cut-off because I was not allowed back out after 6 pm on school nights. I watched whole paychecks and rent money vanish, $20 at a time. I left my friends in 6 inches of snow to go home for dinner and heard someone yelling, and when I turned around, it was his stepfather chasing after me in the snow barefoot to get one more rock. I was completely stunned, and incredibly curious what the high must be like. Curiosity killed the cat. I was 14 the first time I took a hit of crack. The high was instant and very powerful, and very short-lived, so naturally, you need another hit, then another. In a few short months, I was completely broke, barely staying afloat from my weed sales to pay my crack supplier. It was also around this time that one of my customers at school got into trouble and decided to tell the principal about my operation. He began to observe kids dropping their backpacks at my lunch table and coming back for them after they got their food, and then he got the final nail in the coffin when a kid's mom caught him with the gun I sold him, and he told her where he got it. The principal used this to expel me from school. The good news from all of this is that I was broke and severely grounded, so I was no longer able to smoke crack. My parents found a very small Lutheran High School whose principal liked to give 2nd chances to students, and this is where I would eventually graduate from.

Towards the end of sophomore year, I had grown tired of only making $10 a week mowing the grass, and so I searched out and secured a cocaine supplier. A friend then took me to a small 2-unit apartment building and introduced me to 2 strippers and their boyfriends, and I began to make sales daily.

One of those days, I was in the bathroom with the door ajar, getting it ready to sell, when a man walked in and asked to look at what I had. He rolled his eyes and asked if I wanted to make some real money. We took a drive to one of the worst areas in Indianapolis and pulled up to a house with 2 beautiful cars in the drive. Both had extremely expensive paint jobs and rims. The guy we came to see came outside with the biggest gold chain, a diamond watch, and a mouth full of gold teeth. I instantly wanted to be him. I now had a steady supply of crack, and lots of it.

Before I knew it, ounces of crack, lots of LSD, and tons of magic mushrooms were flying out of my hands as fast as I could get them. I was getting good grades at school and playing baseball well enough to make it to college. I carried a gun everywhere I went, and like my supplier, I now wore a ton of jewelry and $2000 worth of gold teeth in my mouth. I, of course, would hide it all when I went home so my parents would not see it. I had life by the balls, and pride came before the fall.

For a 17-year-old kid, I was *"rich"* and was also gaining recognition for baseball. I let the arrogance get to me and thought I could smoke a joint with a little crack in it and be ok.

In the blink of an eye, I was right back to smoking it, and lots of it. To replace the money I was losing, I began robbing other dealers to make sure those closest to me did not catch on. My grades weren't great, and baseball stats were not what they were just a year before, and little did I know my senior year was shaping up to be horrific. We had a play group show up and do a play about addicts in rehab, and they were terrific. I led a standing ovation, and this did not sit well with one of my fellow students, who made a phone call to the principal and said, *"Speziale sells drugs to students at school,"* and hung up.

The principal gave me a chance to clear my name by submitting to a 90-day hair follicle drug screen. The results floored my parents. I failed for everything you can imagine. My parents had me see a counselor and take drug tests once a month at my doctor's office. I had another hair follicle test 90 days later in May, and if I failed, I didn't graduate, which meant I would not be attending college.

In April, I was set up by a so-called friend during a deal. I was beaten in the head with a baseball bat and a tire iron for a $150 bag of mushrooms, a gold chain, and a case of CDs.

Then came the month of February, when I lost 3 friends. The one I was closest to was shot to death for defending a girl who was being assaulted by her 15yr old boyfriend. I went back to smoking crack. I was passing my drug tests at the doctor's office by using a classmate's pee, but I knew I was going to fail my hair follicle test.

The day came. I was to take that test, but when I got to school, there were news crews everywhere. Turned out my baseball coach/English teacher had been having sexual relations with a 14-year-old student when his wife was out of town. The parents of that student removed her and asked the principal not to say anything. They were moving out of state and did not want the public to know what had happened. My coach was suspended, and being the good man my principal was, he did not report it. That student moved to another state and told the story to her therapist, who reported the crime. My principal was fired, and I graduated from school. What a horrific way to be blessed.

My mother wanted me to attend Wabash College in Crawfordsville, Indiana. I had never heard of it, but she said it was a great opportunity, so I agreed. All I cared about was being able to continue playing baseball. She failed to mention it was the last all-male school in the country. College was a wonderful experience, at least for a while. I was not around crack and was supplying the college with marijuana and psychedelics. Freshman year came and went, and summer was spent back home working to have money for school but spending it on crack every weekend.

Then sophomore year is when it all went to shit. That summer, my high school sweetheart ended up pregnant, and when I came back to school, we had our own place with the baby, and honestly, life was great. My grades were better than ever, I wasn't using hard drugs, and I absolutely loved being a father, but didn't notice how unhappy she was.

One night, I came home from a study session to find her and my daughter were gone, and a note saying she still wanted to be together, but she had moved back in with her parents. Hurt, alone, and an addict doesn't go well together.

I had begun doing business with a beautiful tattoo artist from town, and it grew into more than just friends, but she noticed fast that the coke was a problem and insisted I stop. I agreed because I had already become very good at hiding my addictions.

Then 9-11 happened. Something so far from Indiana, but the repercussions it had in my life were catastrophic. The Mexican border was suddenly very tight, and large shipments like marijuana were not getting across, but the smaller ones like cocaine were. So that was the product we were selling or trying to sell before I did it all.

One night, trying to come down from the high, I ate a handful of Xanax, went to the fraternity, and started chugging rum. That is my last memory from that night. I was woken up by my lady, passed out on a couch at the frat house. I was covered in white house paint, my ankle was huge and swollen, and my pockets were full of items that were not mine. I had no clue what happened, but wasn't worried about it until I got the phone call later in the evening. Apparently, an altercation began after paint ended up on someone's car from another frat house. It ended with me hitting them with the paint can, and then stomped them with slippers on, hence the paint on me and the swollen ankle. I was kicked out of school and had a restraining order from the premises.

The next few years were spent screwing up and then fixing the money. Jail time for a DUI, and then a warrant for skipping court, loss of contact with my child, and more drug use. My lady kicked me out, and I don't remember much from the next year, until sobering up in jail. When I got out, we got back together, and I was on house arrest, so I held a job and was sober. It was during this time that we had a house fire and lost everything we owned, and found out we were pregnant. That was a whirlwind that set me on a good course that lasted some time.

Before my 2nd daughter was born, I obtained my real estate license, illicit sales were doing well, and I had lost all desire to do coke, because it turned out that meth was way better. It was amazing in the beginning, I had tons of energy, and could appear normal while on it, unlike coke. I also had to hide it from my woman, so I did not get bad on it, well, not immediately. Real estate came naturally to me, and I was doing well in that business, but was not putting forth much effort because the money was better in the illegal sales world. The relationship I had with the mother of my 2nd child was not a great one. There was fighting, there was cheating, but the positive outweighed the negative in my opinion, at least until my daughter was about 3. It was at this time that I decided to move out so that my daughter did not grow up thinking that was a normal example of a relationship. I moved into the home of my next relationship, and things were great.

I left the real estate world in 2007 when it was clear the market was going to collapse, and went into life and health insurance. I began selling policies to the people I knew who had money to spare and who liked turning money into more money. Due to this, I was doing extremely well, and after just 6 weeks in the business, I was promoted to sales manager and was now making commissions off every policy sold by 6 different agents.

I stopped using meth when I left my ex, was making great money with the insurance gig, and even better money with weed. My new girlfriend was against meth, but I found out that Adderall was just like meth. I was trading weed to everyone in town for meth made by scientists, and was eating 300mg a day and still sleeping at night, and life was great.

Then, one by one, things began to disintegrate.

The First piece to fall was my marijuana supplier, who moved back to Mexico, and supply became hard to come by. Then my Adderall sources dried up, and I could barely get out of bed, and to top it off, I got into a sexual harassment situation at work when a husband reported improper behavior involving his wife and me, and this came with a demotion back to sales rep, which left me only making commissions off my sales.

My sales had vanished because of my lack of interest in life from detoxing off the Adderall. To fill that void, I began to eat painkillers to get some energy, and that decision would affect my life in a myriad of ways over the coming years.

By 2010, I left my job due to getting my license suspended, and any profits I was making with the weed I could get ahold of were going to maintain my pain pill addiction that became all-consuming to avoid the awfulness of the withdrawal symptoms. The one thing that I could count on was the support of my woman, but due to my infidelities, not only was I losing that, I was also losing her completely, and I never even noticed. Then I started using heroin when painkillers were not available. This was the final straw, and I was kicked out of the house and lived on various couches over the next few years.

While hopping couches, I became acquainted with a few people who had an endless supply of heroin and meth, and I was able to make some moves for them to keep myself supplied so that I would not be sick. It turned out that the people in charge were 2 inmates who were serving massive sentences in the state prison system.

I was making enough money to live and had enough drugs to stay high, which was bad news because I had graduated to the needle. I spent two years injecting heroin and meth multiple times a day. It was exhausting. If I went 12 hours without, I would begin to get sick, so there was no option but to maintain the circus.

It was around this time that I took on a summer job detasseling corn, made decent money, and began to slow down on the needle. It was at this job that I met what would become the mother of my 3rd child.

At this point, heroin was the main thing I was moving. One night, I left to go into town to be available for as many sales as I could in order to fix my car. I had a room for the night and had planned to party with a friend while making the money I needed, and that is exactly what I did until my phone rang at 5 o'clock that morning. I was extremely high on meth and heroin, with a bunch of both in the room. I did not recognize the number, but I went ahead and answered.

They said, *"Is this Spaz?"*

When I asked who it was, the response was, *"THIS IS THE FBI."*

I laughed and asked again who it was, and was told to look out my window. There was a full tactical assault team, and an all-black RV that said FBI on the side of it. They proceeded to tell me they had a drug indictment with my name on it and wanted me to come out peacefully, so they didn't have to damage the owner's hotel. I was fully clothed but asked for 5 minutes for my friend and me to get dressed. They agreed, and we began to flush the drugs, and I snorted up as much as I could before I walked out.

I was taken to an FBI building and booked with 44 other people from across 5 states. I was charged with using a communication device to facilitate drug trade and was thrilled to find out that it only carried a 3-year maximum sentence. Remember when I mentioned working for guys in prison, moving enough to stay high? Well, this is what that brought me.

After being booked, we were taken to a jail in Henderson, KY, and a week later, I received a letter from my sister who was very angry with me for putting my mother through this when she was already dealing with my older brother being diagnosed with lung cancer. Turned out the family learned of it when it was covered by the Indianapolis news.

When I had my first hearing, my lawyer informed me that since I did not have any felony convictions on my record, I was being released on pretrial probation. I was driven back to Indianapolis and moved in with my brother and nephew to help while he went through chemotherapy.

Now picture an addict who was forced to get clean, who is facing federal prison time, has a brother who was just diagnosed with cancer, and is living in a house where said brother doesn't take his morphine because of the way it makes him feel. I failed my first drug test, and my probation officer told me that, on my arrest, I failed my screen for a *cornucopia of drugs,* and that he wanted to try and help me before locking me up. This meant seeing a counselor once a week, but in my mind, it meant I could continue to fail drug screens.

After multiple screens failed, I was back before a judge, and my lawyer was able to get me one more chance, but as far as my brother was concerned, I was out of chances, and he kicked me out. My lady and I moved to a motel by the car dealership I was working at, and I managed to detox and stay clean, out of jail, and doing well selling cars. This is when my lady decided she wanted another child, and thinking that was a great idea, I stopped using protection. Within a couple of weeks, we had a positive test and were happy, even though I knew I was headed to prison. Crazy, I know.

I was staying away from opiates, and my morphine supply was no longer available. I was doing great at work, and one Friday night, a friend called to say he had liquid acid, which sounded like a great idea even though I had to work the next morning at 8 am.

Big mistake.

The LSD was much stronger than I needed it to be, and I was still in bad shape come 6 am. To come down, I took some pain pills and was able to make it to work. I knew it took 3 days to get opiates out of my system, and yet somehow, I failed my urine screen 5 days later, and this time, they locked me up. I spent the next 2 years behind bars, and when I was released, I was to spend another year in the federal work release downtown Indianapolis.

During my 2 years of incarceration, I was in contact with my woman until she was about 6 months pregnant. That is when the letters stopped getting replies, and the calls began to go unanswered. I found out later that it was due to her having a new man in her life. Within a few months of this happening, my brother lost his battle against cancer, and through all of this. I did not allow any emotion to come out, since I was in a place where showing emotion was not recommended.

Instead, I stayed high on whatever made its way in and locked everything deep down inside. While in work release, we had random drug tests, but they were not testing for Suboxone which is used to help people stay off heroin but if you are not using opiates, it will get you high the same as painkillers. It made me a very energetic, hard-working individual at my job at a large banquet hotel. This did not go unnoticed, and I quickly earned a couple of promotions and was one promotion away from management, which came with a very nice salary, but I had other plans.

The day of my release, I would be not only out of the facility but off probation as well, and that morning at 6 am, I walked out a free man, who was extremely high from the meth I had eaten a few hours prior. I moved in with a friend who lived close to work and enjoyed meth as much as I did. It took less than 2 months to lose my job due to attendance issues, so I was right back to selling. The individual I lived with left me in charge of the townhouse while he went to rehab, and I only had to pay for my food.

When the lease on the townhouse was up, I moved in with my new girlfriend, who was also an addict, and her mother in Lafayette, but we were sober, and we were both working and about to get our own place. I was seeing my son and youngest daughter regularly and was doing well at another car dealership. If you have figured out the pattern by now, then you should know what comes next. She received a large tax check, and we began using recreationally, then daily, and when I noticed we had nearly pissed the money away, I began selling meth and heroin to keep us afloat.

The relationship was far from healthy, and even though money was coming in from her job and my dealing, we refused to pay rent to spite one another and were evicted. She moved to a different town with her mother, and my choice to stay led me right back to prison.

In less than 18 months of selling drugs in Lafayette, they had me on 2 wired buys, and when I went to be arraigned, I was able to read the paperwork and knew exactly who it was that set me up.

It was a close friend of ours who my children called uncle, someone who was with me every day. I was stunned and beyond angry. I told a fellow inmate that I wanted to kill him for setting me up. This individual insisted I didn't want to do that and to really think about the whole situation. Oddly enough, I began to do just that, and I came to realize that he told me, to avoid going to jail, where he would be sick from heroin withdrawal, and that I was the one supplying him with that drug, so I played a role in my own demise. I knew deep down it was probably breaking his heart that he betrayed me in this way, and I decided that when I bonded out, I would reach out to him and tell him I never want to see him again, but that he is forgiven.

However, I never got the chance to do so because when I posted bond, I found out he had died of an overdose. Fifteen years as a heroin addict and had never overdosed, which made me feel that had I been able to tell him he was forgiven, maybe he would still be alive. This affected me and made me come to the decision that when I went to prison, I would stay sober and out of trouble and take that time to figure myself out, but the 9 months between posting bond and getting sentenced were spent the same way I had been living all these years.

My supplier reached out and offered to put me on to help me get money for a lawyer, and the next thing I knew, I had more meth than I ever had access to. That is not a good thing when you know you're going to prison. I partied harder than ever and did not want the party to end, so on the day of my sentencing, I called my attorney to inform him my car had broken down and I needed to reschedule. He told me the judge was leaning towards house arrest, so I had to get there. No way was I walking into court that day, so a warrant was issued for my arrest. I believe my life on the run lasted all of 10 days before I was arrested and racked up a possession charge to add to everything. The prosecution offered what seemed like a good deal, and then the judge proceeded to max me out on every charge, giving me 7 years with only one year suspended.

A couple of months later, I was on the bus headed to my new home, but I was still dedicated to staying clean and figuring myself out, but in no way was I ever expecting a spiritual awakening to occur, one that would transform my entire being, my life, my future, and hopefully the futures of many others.

My plan was simple: to stay clean, stay out of trouble, and join programs, but I had no clue how to truly fix myself, because I was an addict who did not know what the cause of my addiction was. I did not go through trauma or abuse and was clueless to the why of my being an addict.

One day, while looking at book titles in the library, one caught my attention: **The Hidden Face of God**. I read the back of it, and it turned out to be written by a MIT graduate physicist, and it was detailing all the new discoveries in quantum physics and microbiology and showing where these discoveries were talked about in ancient religious and philosophical writings, such as the Bible and the Upanishads.

By the time I finished that book, my soul was set ablaze, and now I needed more information. I began reading every bit of religious and philosophical writing that I could find from around the world. A whole new concept of what the real me truly is began to take shape.

Then someone noticed me reading a book on Buddhism and invited me to attend the Buddhist Sangha or church service, and I made sure I was on the list for the next week. It was at this service that I meditated for the first time. A guided meditation for the healing of the inner child. I didn't know what to expect since my childhood was not close to ideal family-wise, and since I had never meditated.

As I was visualizing the meditation, I realized my cheeks were wet with tears, and then the guy next to me began sobbing. This meditation brought 2 things from my subconscious and shined a light on them.

The first thing was that I didn't really know my father. All I knew was what others had told me, and of course, you are only going to tell a youngster the good things about the parent they lost. It also showed me that I was hurting deeply from not having contact with my young son for over 2 years.

When I got back to the dorm, I called my mother and told her I needed her to write me a letter and tell me everything about my father, the good, the bad, and the ugly. She did this, and it was an incredible experience to finally get to know my father at the age of 39.

Then I got in contact with my son's mom, and she was open to me rebuilding that relationship.

The difference I felt was immediate. A huge weight was gone, and so I decided I was going to meditate for 5 minutes at the beginning of every day and the end of every night. To my knowledge at that time, meditation was the holding of a thoughtless mind, which I learned quickly was impossible. Thankfully, in some Buddhist texts, I found that an empty mind is the goal, but may take years to achieve. The actual point is to practice observing your thoughts. Simply witness them without judgment, let them go, and bring the focus back to the breath. Over time, the gap between thoughts grows larger, and you spend more time in the only time that is real, the eternal now. By witnessing thoughts, a couple of things happen. You start to become aware of your thoughts in your day-to-day life, and when a thought comes that you do not want to continue with, such as getting high, you can switch to things you are grateful for and begin to control the mind. This began to set me free from the worst prison I have ever been in, the prison in my head. The other thing it does is it creates a knowing that you are not your thinking mind or your body, because you cannot be both the witness to something and the something you are witnessing. Amid the most negative place on earth, I was able to begin and end each day with something peaceful and beautiful, and then the unimaginable began to happen; my perspectives on everything began to change.

Up until this point in life, my views on women were the more the merrier, and I was known for cheating on every woman I had ever been involved with. I never thought twice about it. I can honestly say that the thought of being loyal never crossed my mind. I knew that I was no longer going to have casual sex and that if I were to be in another relationship, I would be completely loyal. It made no sense to me how that shift happened, but I credited it to meditation.

Then came the shift in how I viewed people in general. I found myself looking around at my fellow inmates and being amazed at the amount of intelligence, artistic ability, and musical talent there was behind those walls. This made me realize that most of them were there due to addiction, and I had spent my whole life victimizing these types of people for my own gain. This caused a dark night for my soul, and now I had this overwhelming urge to help people like them, and the non-profit foundation began to take shape in my mind.

Around this time, it was the height of COVID, and what a strange time to be in prison. They stopped all church services, programs, and the 12-step meetings, and people who had been clean for some time began to fall apart, but not me. I took this time to begin outlining and planning the foundation and was blessed to be in a dorm with a few guys from my city who had caught murder sentences nearly 25 years earlier. The guys I used to look up to, and they were telling me what life was like in top-level prisons for decades, and that if it were possible to rewind time, things would have been done very differently. This made me realize that had they told me these horrific stories when I was 12, maybe I would have listened,

That is when the idea of *PreHab* took root in my mind. To have guys like them, the ones who the young thugs would see as credible, tell them what they witnessed in prison and how not everyone survives. *PreHab* to avoid the need for rehab later in life.

I completed the 6-month program and decided to file for a sentence modification, and the judge granted me a hearing. I told him that prison gave me a unique opportunity, one that most people do not get because they do not go to prison, and most of the ones who do, do not utilize the gift. That gift was time, time away from bills, women, the world altogether, time to simply work on myself. I finished my little speech by telling him that I just wanted a chance to thank him for sending me to prison, that it had changed me, and now I had a real chance to live life and help others. He granted my modification but said it would take some time to calculate when my outdate would be.

I continued meditating twice a day and reading books about nonprofits. Through these meditations, I was finally made aware of where my addiction came from. I realized who I truly was, and that person was caring, sensitive, and absolutely loves to help others in any way he can, but the created version of me was living a life of crime, violence, selfishness, and everything that comes from a life of darkness. You cannot be 2 completely different individuals rolled into one without causing a schism within, and it was that fracture between the real me and who I had become that I was running from by staying high. Now I was seeing the world clearly, I felt light and whole, and was only thinking the thoughts I wanted to think. Had I not had that epiphany, the fiasco that was my release would have sent me right back into addiction.

After a month had passed, I sent a letter to the courts asking when my outdate would be. Then, 2 weeks after I sent the letter, on a Friday, the guard called my name over the loudspeaker and said to pack up all my things, I was *'immediate release.'*

My head began to spin. I said my goodbyes and went to the admin building, and while they were doing the paperwork, I asked if they were taking me to work release. I was told to report there the following Monday. They dropped me in Indianapolis at my parents' house, but they were in Arizona. I was able to see my brother and sister, then spent Saturday night with my daughter, and Sunday night was spent in a hotel in Lafayette.

I reported to work release Monday, only to find out it was to set my intake appointment, which was 2 weeks later. I could not believe they didn't inform me that I would need to find somewhere to stay for 2 weeks. I originally was set to do house arrest at my girlfriend's, but she broke things off a couple of weeks before I was released. I called her at work, completely stressed out. Thankfully, she came and picked me up, and I reached out to a friend who had built a great life since his release from prison 5 years prior and asked if I could stay there until my intake date. He said yes as I knew he would, and we began heading to Crawfordsville. When we arrived, I noticed people there who I knew were addicts, and when I inquired, he informed me he took over where I had left off, and that's when I noticed mass quantities of meth and heroin on the desk in the other room. I was very worried, not about using but about the 30-year sentence I would receive if the cops showed up. I made some phone calls and got a ride back to Lafayette, where I proceeded to couch hop until a good friend got me a room for 5 days.

What was truly astonishing is that while discussing the foundation with my friends in prison, I had said I wanted to be able to help people coming home by providing the basics so they do not have to go around the same people and situations that led to their arrests, and then I was face to face with that very scenario. A few months later, that friend was raided by the cops, posted bond, and then died of an overdose, with his daughters bearing the weight of his choices.

The years since I have been home have been incredible. I am not sure how to put it into words, but I will do my best.

I spent a few months in work release and was employed at an auto manufacturer, where I still work today. When I had enough saved, I was able to transition out of work release and onto house arrest in a one-room apartment I refer to as *"The Shoebox,"* and 4 years later, that is where I am writing this story.

I spend as much time with my family and my children as possible, and seeing on their faces that they trust what they see and that it no longer hurts them to love me is true bliss. The free time that I do have is spent either in nature or building the nonprofit. When I say this is what my soul's purpose is, that is not a belief; it is truth.

My nephew, who recently graduated from Purdue for web design, had our website up in no time.

A friend from high school, who I had not spoken to since graduation, became a lawyer and a founder of a nonprofit. He guided me through state and federal licensing. I reconnected with people I knew from my life in the streets who had also found recovery, and my board of directors took shape.

The foundation is named **Stephanie's Courage A PreHab Organization**. The name is one I take great pride in.

Stephanie was a good friend of mine for many years and a fellow addict. She had been through hell in life. As a teen, she was the one to find her mother and her stepfather dead from a murder suicide. She was one of the people I never expected to embrace recovery, and when I got home, I found out that she was indeed sober and had been for some time. I was overjoyed until she told me that shortly after getting clean, she was diagnosed with terminal cancer. The mind of an addict makes excuses over every negative in life as a reason to get high, and often over positive events as a celebration, and here she was, faced with a situation that no one would blame her for using again, and yet she remained sober. She even had other people control her pain meds so she could not numb herself to the coming fate. To me, this was a testimony of strength and courage. We do what we do in honor of her.

About 2 years after my release, I was reading a book by a man named Ivan Antic, and I had goose bumps because he was describing the changes that come from meditation, yoga, breathwork, etc. What he calls energetic practices. He explained that we have chakras, and each one is like a miniature brain that handles different aspects of life. When we go through trauma, ingest poisons, eat toxic foods, etc., they become out of balance, and on a day-to-day basis, our thinking mind eats a lot of this energy as well as our digestive system, because we have been convinced that we are supposed to eat 3 times a day. The simple act of meditation frees up energy the mind is using, and the chakras begin to function properly.

The first thing people tend to notice is a change in views on sex because the first center that begins to function is the 2nd chakra or sexual center. Then, when the energy begins to move from the 3rd center, which is our will power, we stop using our will for selfishness and start using it to create and to help others. This is exactly what happened to me when I began to meditate daily. Then, when I came home, I detoxed my body thoroughly and began practices designed to move that energy, like fasting and kundalini yoga, and I was not prepared for what happened when I had been doing these for an extended period. That energy flooded my heart center, and it came with a massive sensation of bliss, chills, tears, and an overwhelming love for every person, every creature, and all of nature. If this energy continues to rise, it reaches the throat center, and you cannot shut up about it. You want to tell everyone, and when you do get to talk about it, at least for me, it makes you high. I have been teaching mediation and healing techniques to inmates for 2 years now, and I warn my class that they're going to watch me get higher than I ever did on drugs.

When you feel love for every being and see God in everything, life is truly beautiful, and it flows. Even when life doesn't seem to be going your way, I have learned it is always in our best interest.

For example, a few months ago, after a workout, I had a knot form in the muscle between my neck and shoulder, and it decided to pinch a nerve. Driving backwards on my fork truck at work was very painful, and I could not meditate for more than a couple of minutes. I felt out of balance spiritually and in constant pain. After a month had passed, I posted about it on Facebook, and a friend sent me x-rays of his spine, pictures of a car crash, and contact information of an acupuncturist, and told me she was the only doctor who was able to restore mobility to his back. I made an appointment, and while she worked, I told her about my foundation, and she told me she loves helping people in recovery. It turned out that one of her employees was in jail for pills, and I was able to assist in getting sober living lined up upon his release. Then came my 2nd appointment, where she offered me a few rental properties to turn into our own sober living homes. A 5–10-year goal was now sped up to 12 months. I burst out in deep laughter, and when she asked what was funny, I told her that I now know why the universe pinched my nerve and why it took so long to heal. I left her office that day pain-free.

I wonder how many of you read that and thought, *"What luck!"* There is no such thing as luck. We are meant to go through everything that comes our way. Every poor decision I made, every drug I ingested, every arrest that happened, all of it, was meant for me. It built me, piece by piece, tear after tear, into who I am today, and with the purpose I now have, and had I not gone through every bit of it, I would not have the passion or ability to help those in need.

Stephanie's Courage Organization is blazing a new path in the world of recovery. We want people to learn to heal from their traumas and how to connect to the soul that lives within each of us. To teach them through meditation how to control the mind, while strengthening the influence of the eternal witness within. When this happens, your spirit is in the driver's seat, and decisions that go against your soul become increasingly impossible to make. Couple these practices with healing from past traumas, and eating healthy with a clean body and exercising can turn these tortured souls into true beacons of light for others to see. We don't want to just help people stay clean; we want to help them heal and transform in such a profound way that they feel compelled to look behind them and extend a hand to pull others up to the heights they have reached.

Today, I am more than 7 years clean, I am an honest and loyal man, and all I want for my remaining years in this body is to help as many people as possible wake up to how wonderful this mysterious thing called life can be. If you take anything away from my story, I hope it's a different perspective on addicts and criminals. They are all divine beings with endless potential. They simply have allowed life, trauma, and society to cloud the mirror of their soul. When those mirrors are clean, who knows what the future holds for them, and how much good they can bring into this world. Thank you for your time and interest in what I call My Life.

PETER SPEZIALE

Drug Prevention Advocate, Personal Transformation Coach

Peter "Matt" Speziale is the founder of **Stephanie's Courage**, a nonprofit dedicated to drug prevention, personal transformation, and supporting individuals impacted by addiction and incarceration. After spending 25 years involved in drug trafficking and addiction—choices that led to lost opportunities and time in both federal and state prison—Peter experienced a profound spiritual awakening that changed the course of his life.

Through reflection and the wisdom of others he met while incarcerated, he developed a passion for helping young people avoid the path he once took and for helping those in prison use their time to rebuild their lives. Today, through Stephanie's Courage, Peter works to educate youth about the real dangers of drugs and to support individuals seeking a second chance and a better future.

Connect with Peter
Facebook: Peter Speziale
Website - www.scprehab.com

THE STORY OF ADRIENNE BENDER

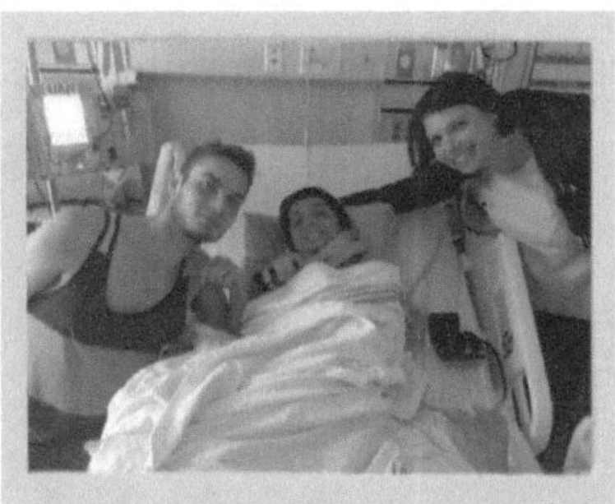

RAINBOWS AFTER THE STORM

I used to think the meaning of life was something you discovered all at once, like a final answer waiting at the end of a long road. Now I think it reveals itself in fragments, often during moments you never asked for. The ones that break you open. My life has been shaped by those moments…by loss, by endurance, by the quiet insistence that I keep going even when I wasn't sure how.

As a child, I wondered why I was here. I sensed there was a larger pattern unfolding, though I could never quite see it clearly. That feeling followed me into adulthood, growing sharper with each turning point.

I finished high school in two years, stacking summer school and correspondence classes while working two part-time jobs. I learned early how to be self-reliant. Growing up in a split family made that unavoidable. I planned to start university in the fall, but a brief romance altered the trajectory of my life. When I found out I was pregnant, I chose to postpone school and raise my child on my own. I didn't ask for help. I believed that taking responsibility meant carrying everything myself.

That belief followed me into my first marriage. I married young and had another child shortly afterward. The marriage was strained from the beginning, and I learned to manage without support… emotionally, practically, quietly. When my youngest was eight months old, I started nursing school. I told myself I was doing what I had to do. By the time I finished, the marriage had collapsed under the weight of everything I was holding. I became a single mother again, this time to two children.

Not long after, I met my second husband. When he lost his job, I let him move in quickly. Caring for others felt natural to me. For a while, life felt stable. We traveled. Our blended family fit together easily.

Then my eldest, Kyler, was twelve and beginning to slip away from me.

At first, it was small…experimentation, curiosity. Then it wasn't. His behavior changed, his moods darkened, and the house began to feel tense in a way I couldn't name yet. When his substance use escalated, I quit my job to focus entirely on him. I pulled him out of school, homeschooled him, found counselors and psychiatrists. For six months, I stayed close, watching and waiting, hoping vigilance would be enough.

When he returned to school, I allowed myself to believe we had turned a corner.

A week later, my younger child, Mackenzie, was diagnosed with AML leukemia.

She had been complaining of a sore arm, something that didn't seem urgent until it was. Suddenly, we were living in hospital rooms. Because I wasn't working, I stayed with her through long admissions and invasive treatments. Kyler began to unravel again. This time, I let my mother take him in. It felt like a failure, even though it wasn't.

Mackenzie recovered fully after months of treatment. When Kyler returned from rehab, our family was briefly whole again. Soon after, my husband lost his job, and I returned to work, long hours, 60-hour weeks, doing what I had always done to keep us afloat.

The marriage suffered. I was rarely home. Kyler turned eighteen and became harder to reach - angrier, riskier. One night, while I was at work, my husband and I argued over text. When I got home, he was gone. Later, a message appeared on my phone: *I'm gone.* His number and email were deleted. My car was abandoned at my sister's house, door open. He took nothing but his passport.

For a long time, I believed he had killed himself.

I kept working. Kyler brought dangerous people into the house, and for the first time, I chose safety over saving him. I asked him to leave. I couldn't sell the house or the vehicles without my husband's signature, and he was unreachable. I managed anyway.

Five years after remission, Mackenzie's cancer returned.

There was no time to prepare. We had to move cities for treatment. When I reached out to my sister-in-law, I learned my husband had emptied our savings and moved to Vietnam. For the first time in my life, I asked for help without apology. Friends, family, and charities made it possible for us to leave.

This time was harder. I declined visitors. I wanted to protect Mackenzie from being seen in pain. I stayed with her through complications that nearly killed her, through procedures no child should endure.

When we returned home, my husband reappeared to finalize the divorce. I sold the house, hopeful that something might finally ease. Instead, Mackenzie's body began rejecting the stem cell transplant. Between work and hospital stays, life narrowed to survival.

I moved in with a man who had two young children, hoping to give Mackenzie a sense of family again. After years of fighting, her doctor asked if she would want CPR if her heart stopped. She said no. She was tired.

Kyler was deep in addiction again. When I told him she was dying, he ran to the hospital in stocking feet. Mackenzie died while I rubbed her feet.

Grief didn't arrive all at once. It came in tasks, expectations, and quiet endurance. The man I lived with expected me to resume caretaking, to return to work, to function. I did. I didn't know how not to.

Four months later, my father called. He had leukemia — the same kind that took Mackenzie. Six weeks after his diagnosis, he died from an infection. I planned another funeral while caring for my grandfather, whose dementia had worsened. When I asked my aunt for help, she declined. The pandemic followed soon after. Eventually, I placed my grandfather in long-term care. Six weeks later, he died too.

Kyler overdosed not long after. I brought him home again, on the condition that he seek treatment. There were police visits, emergency rooms, fear I couldn't name without shaking. Then something shifted. He stabilized. He worked. He applied to college. He wanted to become an addiction counselor. He was sober. He was proud of himself.

A month after he moved into student housing, I received a string of texts. He had been beaten. Days later, I saw a post online: *RIP Kyler*.

I went to his apartment. It was a homicide investigation. I wasn't allowed into his room until the coroner removed his body. He had been doing well. He had been trying.

I lost both my children.

What remains of me is not the woman who believed strength meant doing everything alone. Grief dismantled that version of myself completely. In its place is someone quieter, more open, more willing to be held.

The losses did not offer answers. They did not resolve into meaning. But they taught me this: life does not stop being sacred because it is fragile. The rainbows I see now do not erase the storms. They appear beside them—brief, unexpected, real. And some days, that is enough.

ADRIENNE BENDER

Grief Coach, Author, Health Therapist

Adrienne Bender is a registered psychiatric nurse, certified grief coach, and author of The Almost Miracle Years. Through her deeply personal journey of enduring the unimaginable loss of both her children, she has become a compassionate voice for healing, hope, and resilience.

With remarkable vulnerability and warmth, Adrienne shares her lived experiences to help others navigate grief, find meaning in suffering, and rediscover purpose after loss. Her work is rooted in the belief that even in the midst of heartbreak, life can still be honored and celebrated. Through her writing, coaching, and speaking, Adrienne offers comfort, understanding, and guidance to those walking through their own journeys of grief.

Connect with Adrienne
FB - adrienne.reimer.9
IG - @ady.bends

THE STORY OF HEATHER AND MICHAEL COTTOM

"THE WARRIOR"

Heather's Perspective

My first real recollection of there being something wrong was when I had awoken from my C-section, emergency C-section that is, and I could hear my ex-husband on the phone with someone saying, *"They're gonna take him down to Children's Hospital of Buffalo for further evaluation. They think it's something with his heart."* I could hear my husband on the phone with someone.

My post-surgical anesthesia wore off in an instant, and I shot out of bed like a cannon. *"What's wrong ?"* I said.

He explained that they had to take Michael down to the Children's Hospital because he had some *"issues"* after he was born. He came out cyanotic and had trouble breathing. Last I knew, I was in labor, and I had a bunch of doctors looking at the EKG machine. My doctor came in and immediately said, *"We gotta do a C-section immediately!"*

"Get her down to the OR stat!"

No, that's not what scared me. I assumed it was something like an umbilical cord wrapped around his neck or something that they routinely see. They rushed me down to the OR, where they tried to give me an epidural.

My doctor shouted out, *"We don't have time! Knock her out now!"*

I mean, I was a little scared, but I had already had two healthy babies and a miscarriage; I had been through a lot. I figured it was just something routine, and everything would work itself out.

I was barely awake when I heard my husband on the phone; he was talking so quietly that I could barely hear him. I made out him saying, *"They're not sure yet, they're transporting him to Children's for further testing."*

I jumped out of bed. I wasn't sure that I was hearing anything correctly at this point. A nurse had come in while I was in recovery with my husband and explained that there just happened to be a nurse from Children's on rotation at the time when Michael was in the OR with us, and as soon as he came out, they recognized that *"classic"* blue cyanotic color, flagging the possibility of a heart condition. At this point, he was put on oxygen, and they had to transport him to the Children's in the Neonatal Ambulance.

Luckily, my husband knew people from the neonatal transport unit who would be taking Michael down to Buffalo Children's Hospital. They technically weren't supposed to, but they popped in real quick so that I could see him before they whisked him away. He was beautiful. He had so much hair all over his head and had actual sideburns! (The nurses nicknamed him Baby Elvis) He was in an incubator, so I couldn't even touch him. I was so sad, but I knew that time was of the essence

Because of having a C-section, they wouldn't let me go with him, which, of course, made me so upset. I wanted to be there. I wanted to sit with him every minute of the day to make sure that everything that needed to be done was done. I told my whole family don't come up and see me, if anything, go to Children's and sit with him. Ask questions and see what they're doing.

It literally drove me insane, not sitting there, unable to really get up and walk around. I was in so much pain from the C-section, yet that little fire underneath me kept blazing. I needed to be with Michael. I have been called *"helicopter mother"*, and to some people they might be an insult, but you know what? I knew what I had to do and where I had to be. I missed all my kids so much; my oldest, Emily, was 6, Matt was 2, and especially my youngest, Michael. Everybody was concerned, and everybody wanted answers.

The next day, after a sleepless night, I decided I had to get out of that hospital and get to Michael. I did not care about myself or how I felt. I knew he needed to be with his mama.

The Hospital staff kept telling me, *"You just had a C-section, you really need to rest. Michael is in good hands."* I asked the nurse to call my doctor and ask for release papers. The nurse grudgingly went back to the station to call my doctor. She told me she couldn't get a hold of him to write the papers; he was out golfing. I had told her I really don't care who signs the papers or if anyone signs the papers, I was leaving that afternoon. Papers or not. I had to go to Children's to see my son.

When they finally released me, I made my husband drive me immediately up to see Michael. I had him drop me off at the door so I could go right up in the NICU to see him. When I got upstairs, I had to sign in and scrub up. The nurse was amazed that I was not only out of the hospital but able to get up to the NICU that fast. She immediately got me a chair, and I was able to sit by Mike's incubator.

The first thing I noticed was that he was on oxygen. He had a lot of wires and stickers with things that I had no idea about. Little did I know that I would eventually become an expert on all this. Not that I wanted to, but because I had to.

We found out later that day that Michael was born with a congenital heart defect called hypoplastic right heart syndrome, HRHS for short. Essentially, it's half a heart. Luckily enough, Michael was left with the good side of the heart, the pumping side. The doctors all told me if you're going to be born with a hypoplastic heart, this is the one you want. Oddly enough, I felt like we had won the lottery.

He would require open-heart surgery immediately, something that our local Children's Hospital in Buffalo could not do because there were no heart surgeons there. The closest heart surgeon was an hour away. At Golisano Children's Hospital in Rochester, New York. They were planning on taking him the next day. He needed heart surgery immediately, or he wouldn't make it.

Once we got to Rochester, we were able to talk to many different people on the pediatric cardiology team. With Mike's diagnosis, he'd need a set of 3 surgeries over time at crucial points in his life. The first surgery he was to have was the *"The Bi-Directional Glen"*. This surgery is the most complex and crucial. In this surgery, Dr. Alfieris would place a shunt to allow for more blood flow to his heart and reroute the plumbing in Mike's heart.

The surgeon would combine the nonworking ventricle with the working ventricle to make two large chambers, so instead of the four chambers that most people have in a healthy heart, Michael would be down to two larger chambers, and he would then be considered a single ventricle heart patient. Essentially, the oxygenated and unoxygenated blood mix in the same chamber. Often, single ventricle heart patients will have a low pulse ox, due to the fact that their blood is not oxygen-rich like yours and mine. This is actually what alerted a nurse from the Children's Hospital in Buffalo. Dr. Alfieris would also place a stent to improve the blood flow to his heart.

The surgery would start at a very early 7 AM and could last anywhere from 4-7 hours. Dr. Alfieris, the surgeon, and his NP, Gina, explained the whole process and what would take place. He would have to be put on an ECMO machine, which would pump his blood throughout his body so that they could work on his heart, essentially a bypass machine. The thought of a machine keeping my son alive was so frightening. This doctor was working on this tiny baby's heart; they explained it's the size of a golf ball.

While surgery took place, we waited in the waiting room right outside, where Mike would be after surgery, in the

NICU. Time felt like it was standing still. I couldn't read, I couldn't watch TV. All I could do was pace down the hall and back into the waiting room. Finally, after what seemed like forever, they had called to say that Mike was under anesthesia and successfully on the ECMO machine. The ECMO was doing the work of his heart while surgery was being performed on his fragile heart.

Hours later, Gina came out and said that they were finished and he would be in recovery for a while, and then we'd be able to see him after about an hour. After about an hour and a half, I was getting really, really antsy. I had no idea why we weren't back there yet. I wanted to knock on the door of the neck and see if they had maybe forgot about us. I wasn't sure at that point. My husband kept saying he's fine, stop worrying. Just let them do whatever they gotta do, and then they'll call us.

In the waiting room, we were sitting in was a long skinny fish tank the whole length of the room, so you could see the hallway through the fish tank. All of a sudden, I see them running down the hall, pushing a bed, and I see a lady standing on the edge of the bed as they're wheeling it, giving the patient CPR, and giving him oxygen. I did not see any faces. I didn't see the patient. I just saw the blur of them moving past the waiting room. I stood up to look out the door of the room, but it was too late; they were already on an elevator. Something hit me like a brick; it's like I knew before I actually knew.

"That was Michael," I said.

My husband looked at me like I had 6 eyeballs. *"Calm down, it was NOT Mike, just sit down and wait till they call us back."*

Approximately 45 minutes later, Gina appeared in the waiting room with a look in her eyes. I knew what she was gonna say.

"That was Mike, wasn't it?" I started bawling as she reached down to hug me to confirm what I had already known.

She explained that when he was brought up after surgery, his numbers weren't as good as they should have been after having an extensive surgery as he had. His stats were low and never came up like they normally do with Alfieris' kids. She stated they had to take him back down and open his chest up, and they were doing another surgery on him. She also explained that Dr. Alfieris felt like the shunts that he used normally in a kid of Mike's size weren't big enough. They had gone back into place a bigger shunt.

In the middle of all this, half of the lights in the hospital went out. I had no idea what was going on. Freaking out would be an understatement. The hospital's TV in the waiting room was still working even though many of the lights in the hospital were out. We all sat in the waiting room watching the

TV and found out that half of New York State and parts of northeast Ohio and Pennsylvania were all out of power due to a total Grid failure.

Now I had no idea what the heck that meant, nor did I honestly care at this point; my concern was my baby, my not even a week old baby that was being operated on. Gina ran up to explain that the OR's are always on generator backup. Those rooms always had power, along with the patient rooms, due to the generator setup.

I also need to explain to you that Dr. Alfieris is a very well-known doctor in the Rochester area and also does surgeries in the Syracuse area, about an hour away from Rochester. He has a reputation as an excellent surgeon who does not mess up frequently. A lot of heart kids from Buffalo end up in Rochester, Cleveland, Philadelphia, and other well-known hospitals that are known for their cardiac excellence. We had a time crunch issue on our hands, and we heard that Dr. Alfieris was one of the best. We didn't have time to travel or just second-guess ourselves. Dr. Alfieris does so many delicate, intricate surgeries, sometimes 12 hours long, that he does not drive himself. He has a car that drives him where he needs to be. Later, we'd come to find out that Dr. Alfieris's car was stuck in traffic on the Rochester inner Loop downtown, and the driver couldn't get to the hospital, which is why Dr. Alfieris was there, thank the good Lord to do Michael's surgery.

Later, we would be told that if Dr. Alfieris wasn't at the hospital and there wasn't a blackout, Michael might not have made it through that night. Everything happens for a reason, I told myself. I was thanking God the driver got stuck. Hours later, when we were able to go back to the cardiac unit and FINALLY see him, I was not ready at all to see all the IVs and the machines and the noises. He had about 12 IVs, and I could hear the beeping of the machine that measured his heart rate, a sound that still triggers Michael and me to this day.

The nurse explained everything he was hooked up to and what it measured. It was so horrifying to look at. All the nurses in the cardiac unit came by to see Michael because, in everyone's eyes, he was a miracle baby. It was a miracle that Dr. Alfieris was stuck at the hospital. A nurse came by the next shift and said he's not my patient, but I wanted to see the baby that flatlined, and what a tough little guy he must be. My head started spinning out of control. I got an immediate migraine. I had no idea that he flatlined. No one mentioned this at all to us. It wouldn't have mattered in the wrong of things, but it really caught me off guard because they had to go in twice for his surgery.

They could not close his chest up. He had a special tape on his chest from the same people who make scotch tape, a special adhesive to put over his wounds. The nurses would come in every day to change it, and the nurse said to me one day, *"You might not want to watch, I need to change his dressing."*

At this point, I was not about to leave this baby for a minute. I hated going to the bathroom or even eating because I did not want to leave his side for obvious reasons. As she changed the dressing, you could see his heart beating inside his chest. It would probably gross some people out, but that was my baby, my tough warrior. He had been through so much already, I couldn't imagine what life had in store for him. I stayed at the hospital with him for over a month. My mom would come up and stay with him and sleep there while I went home and got rest and saw my other kids. My husband, on the other hand, wasn't very good with this type of thing, so we made him in charge of home.

Mike would be in the hospital for a month. It was terrible. I missed my kids, Emily and Matthew, at home, and when I was home, and my mom or my husband was up with Mike, I was filled with constant worry. I was emotionally and physically spent.

Mike got to go home after a month, and we began to live life and assimilate into a schedule. We had feeding issues because he wasn't able to breathe and nurse at the same time since he only had high 80s oxygen. It was a long year of appointments, testing, and basically allowing Michael to be a baby, which was so hard at times. I was afraid to let him cry too long because it would immediately turn blue like a Smurf, so I picked him up right away. The *"cry out rule"* never applied here. He was delicate in my eyes.

Fast forward to when Michael was 18 months old. He had finally healed up from his heart surgery, thankfully, but something kept bothering me and kept me awake at night. I waited till his check-up and asked his pediatrician about it.

I said, "See *that bump on the front of his forehead? Do we think that's anything to worry about?*"

The doctor assured me it was most likely nothing to worry about. He claimed heart babies often had misshapen skulls due to the fact that they weren't as active as healthy babies. I thought about his answer for the next week or so, and then I decided to do something totally out of the ordinary for me. I decided to look up neurosurgeons at our local Children's Hospital and make an appointment for Michael, unknown to anybody else in my family. My husband at the time, Michael's father, clearly disagreed with me and told me to calm down. It was nothing to worry about; even the pediatrician said it was nothing. I made the appointment with Dr. Li and got in relatively quickly, thank God. I took my mom. She and I went together up to Children's because I knew I would need support. Dr. Li is one of the best neurosurgeons in the Western New York area, which is why I made the appointment with him. Dr. Li knocked on the door, came in, and proceeded to wash his hands as most doctors do. He didn't even get to drying them when he looked at Mike and said, "*Your baby needs major surgery.*"

I said, "*What????*"

I think I would've passed out except for the fact that I was holding Michael. I immediately gave Michael to my mom. Dr. Li went on to explain that the misshapen head wasn't merely a misshapen head; it was much more complex. He explained that Michael had a condition called Craniosynostosis. This condition happens when the plates in the infant's skull close prematurely, causing a bump on the baby's head. In this case, it was in front of Michael's forehead. He went on to explain that a lot of times these babies are put in helmets to help shape their head in a correct manner; however, with Michael being 18 months old already, that was too late, and Dr. Li's opinion would require a lengthy surgery. I told Dr. Li that I would have to get back to him after I explained everything to my husband, who didn't even know I was there

Later that night, I had to explain my day and what had happened to my husband, who had no idea where I was or who I was with. You will later understand why I had to do this. I broke the news to my husband, who literally blew up at me, telling me that. *"Mike was fine and didn't need surgery"*.

Why he felt this way, I don't know. He never even went to a pediatrician appointment with me, as it was. I took all 3 of my kids by myself, or my mom went with me. The conversation continued, and Michael's father told me that we were gonna get a second opinion. which I wholeheartedly agreed with anyway. With Michael having open-heart surgery six months earlier, I wasn't very eager to have another major surgery in the same year. We both agreed that we were gonna take Michael to Strong and Rochester, where he had his heart surgery. I felt very comfortable knowing that they would have answers for us and that the cardiac team would be in the OR if any other operations took place. We went to Strong, and the neurosurgeon there confirmed what we already knew.

Michael had craniosynostosis and needed surgery immediately, as there was a risk that the plates would close and start to affect Michael's brain if the surgery wasn't done. Michael's surgery took place a couple of weeks after our appointment, which was as soon as they could get us in. And let me tell you, it was the longest surgery I had ever seen or any of my family had ever seen. The surgery took 10 hours, and let me tell you guys, the doctor came out at the midpoint of the surgery to reassure us and let us know everything was going OK. The patients tend to lose a lot of blood, and let me just tell you, the doctor in his scrubs was a gruesome sight, which I hope no one needs to see the blood of their own child on their doctor's scrubs. The image will honestly stay with me always.

After surgery, Michael was placed in the NICU. Imagine trying to explain to your 18-month-old baby why his eyes were swollen shut and why he couldn't see anything. It was terrible. It was honestly the most horrific thing I've ever had to go through with my kids. They kept him on morphine, and he was on a breathing tube, sedated to let him rest and heal up a little. It was already decided that I'd stay with Michael and that his dad would go home and be with his brother and sister. I slept on the bench in his room, watching and waiting and hoping that this was gonna be a short stay at Strong. We were there about two weeks before they let us come home.

Poor Michael had sutures in his head from one ear up over his head to the other ear like a zigzag headband. It was terrible. The doctor said they had to make the incision, flip his forehead forward, and put all the bones in his skull together (like mosaic tile), and then sew his incisions together to flatten his forehead out.

During the first couple years of his life, we were heavily involved with early intervention through Erie County. Early intervention was a program in which specialty therapists would come out and help Mike. Speech, Occupational, and Physical Therapy. Michael definitely qualified because he was having trouble reaching any of the typical milestones that babies reach. We had a regular schedule of consistent therapy every day. I had to work, and thankfully, my Mom was home watching Michael. I would never have been able to put him in a daycare. He had PT, OT, and Speech 2x a week. By the end of the week, Michael was exhausted. Took everything out of him. He had a significant speech delay, and by that time, he should have been crawling, babbling, and doing things that we sometimes take for granted that babies do, and he just wasn't doing it. They even started to teach him sign language because they weren't sure that he would be able to talk.

The next couple of years would be full of appointments with specialists locally and in Rochester. Michael continued with his PT, OT, and Speech, and thank God we had wonderful teachers who helped him try to catch up to the milestones that he should be at according to his age. Michael's father decided that he didn't wanna be married anymore and moved out. It was a terrible time for the entire family.

Despite everything, Michael was such a good boy. Sweet, kind, caring, and didn't mind going to the doctor's appointments. Shortly before Michael turned 5, we were given the news that Michael would have to have open-heart surgery #4. You knew it was inevitable, but just hearing those words really felt like a punch in the gut. This little guy was barely five, and look at everything we had been through with him. Our local cardiologist in Buffalo contacted the surgeon's office in Rochester to set up his surgery once again.

The morning of the surgery is still etched in my mind. We left the house at 5 am to make it to Rochester by 6. Michael wore his bright yellow SpongeBob SquarePants Crocs, his favorite pajamas from the movie *"Cars".* As Mike and I maneuvered through the maze of the hospital, I could feel his hand holding me tighter and tighter as we went into the elevator and went down to the basement for the OR waiting room. Michael was nervous. How do you tell a child that's been through so much in such a short span of time what exactly was gonna take place? My heart hurt. I had to keep it all in, and I could not cry in front of him because I knew that would not be a good idea, because he'd start crying too. When we got downstairs, the staff remembered us from when he was a baby there. The cardiac nurses took him back into the pre-operating waiting area, where he put on a tiny gown. I still remember the wallpaper with all the underwater fish and plants on the wall. Seems like we were always in the same room. They did the normal things: blood pressure, height, and weight. All while Michael was clutching his faithful therapy dog Jessie, the same one his sister Emily had put in the incubator five short years ago before Mike's first open heart surgery. Michael took him to every doctor's appointment. Every time Michael was anxious, Jessie was there with him. Jessie is still in Michael's room to this day; he's been very well loved. We've had to do a few surgeries on him, but nevertheless, he still looks pretty good for an old dog.

Rounds of people came in and out. I could barely remember any of their names or what they did. The anesthesiologist came in and told us that Michael would be getting *"happy juice"*. It would make him less anxious until they were able to give him total sedation, which he would need for the surgery. The happy juice kicked in pretty fast. Thankfully, Michael was silly, giggling and laughing uncontrollably. I, however, was getting more nervous because I knew the time I would have to say goodbye to him was drawing near. I wish they had happy juice for the parents

Before I knew it, one of the doctors came back and said, *"Mike, are you ready to go?"* The doctor picked him up without any fuss, tears, or fear. The nurse practitioner told us that I could go up to the fourth-floor waiting room and she would keep me in the loop of what was happening. After an hour, I got a phone call saying that they were just getting started, that Michael was asleep, and that the surgery would be at least 4 to 5 hours. I made a point to never sit in that waiting room where I was when I got the terrible news that Mike had to have 2 surgeries in one day. It was like bad juju for me. Dr. Alfieris wanted to make a hole in the wall between the two chambers, not only to lessen his blood pressure but to help with the mixing of the blood between the two chambers. They also decided to implant a pacemaker as a precautionary measure, just in case it was needed. Thankfully, he weathered this surgery well and was able to stay in the hospital for only a week!

Mike has endured so much, it's honestly unbelievable. He had ENT issues, tonsils and adenoids removed, 4 nose surgeries due to the Craniosynostosis, and the fact that Michael's face is not symmetrical. An endless number of cardiac catheterizations to measure pressures in his heart. This year, Michael will have to have another big surgery. He needs to have a *"Rapid Palate Extension."* He will have to get his upper palate cut and stretched out in order to open up the airway to his nose. Michael has never had a sense of smell. I keep telling him that it could be a good thing or a bad thing!

Despite everything, Michael remains the most generous, sweet, kind, caring human being that you'd ever want to meet. He has hopes of going to school to be a counselor for kids who have special needs, as he knows what it feels like to not have anyone to talk to who has been in his shoes and can understand where they are coming from. I pray that someday Mike will excel in whatever he chooses to do. He knows no matter what, I'll always have his back, and he'll always have mine.

Michael's perspective

My story begins with nurses scrambling as I had just been born; something was wrong. Something that would almost end my life not long after it began.

My heart was deformed. Most people have two ventricles, but I only had one. I literally had half a heart. I would spend the first week of my life being passed around like a hot potato between different hospitals until the next week, when I would have my very first open-heart surgery.

The surgery would appear to be a success until I was in the recovery unit, where I flatlined. The shunt they put in was too small, and I had to go back into the Operating Room for a

2nd heart surgery. Thankfully, this surgery was a success, and I would eventually get to go home.

Home wasn't without conflict as my parents were going through a divorce. My father was not an empathetic person. He left my mom and got remarried shortly after the divorce was final. He and my stepmom would often disregard and downplay my illnesses and disabilities. He would even go so far as to refuse to give me my prescribed medications when I had visitation at his house. He kept telling me, *"I was fixed."* As if I grew half a heart overnight.

As I would do chores, I would naturally get tired due to my heart condition and would need frequent breaks. My father, however, would tell me to stop making excuses and that I'm not as sick as I think I am.

My stepmom was no better; she would often call me **"*retarded*"** because I wasn't good at math and didn't know how to tie my shoes. While the other kids got to walk and get ice cream, I would be stuck there, being forced to do my math with no help. My father would eventually give up his joint custody, emancipate my older brother and me, so he didn't have to pay child support, and granted full custody to my mother.

I would go on to have 2 more open-heart surgeries. A pacemaker was implanted during the last one.

Later that year, I would begin my school career in elementary school. Things were going great, but I would be out sick often. I would have sinus infections on top of sinus infections, and we would not know why until I started middle school.

Middle school is where everything would take a turn, as I would still be out of school for many days. On top of that, I would also be ruthlessly bullied not just by my peers but also by the teachers and administration. I was picked on for being the *"weird"* kid and would be constantly made fun of for my many absences. The school just didn't understand the extent of my disabilities and would refuse to try to understand. They refused to cut me any slack and ignored my IEP constantly.

Everything was a continuous battle. I would later be diagnosed with primary immunodeficiency. My immunologist described it as my immune system being slightly better than that of a person with AIDS. That explained why I kept getting sick, but the school still refused to believe me. An immunologist said that often the thymus gland is taken out during emergency heart surgery. It's directly in front of where they need to operate, so they take it out, not realizing what it does to all us heart kids.

Even when I had a doctor's note, they would still find a way to make it seem like I was home playing Xbox all day. When in reality, I was practically bedridden. One school year, I had 9 documented sinus infections alone. My guidance counselor told my mom that it *"just wasn't possible."* The bullying didn't stop there, as it would eventually evolve into students bodychecking me into the lockers like a hockey player.

On top of that, my father would re-enter the picture as he would make numerous false CPS reports, along with the school, which he secretly called, claiming my mother had Munchausen by proxy. I felt like I was being bullied by everyone. School would somehow take my dad's word over my mom's. My life seemed to be spiraling out of control. My father tried to take my mom to court to try to get custody of my siblings and me. He didn't win. He was only trying to make my mom's life a living hell.

As one CPS case would close, the next one would open. Sometimes the very same day. CPS never believed my dad anyway, but since the call was made, they had to come out; they knew my entire family and me. They would come, fill out the paperwork, and leave. They totally understood what we were all going through. They had a job to do, though, and I totally understand that. What killed me is they kept coming out to see me and my family, who are doing absolutely nothing wrong. Endless cases were never investigated because of the shortage of workers at CPS. That's the kicker of it. They had to investigate my false cases while some kid was getting abused in the city. It was heartbreaking. I didn't understand any of it, between the endless bullying and the possibility of being forced to live with my abusive father. I had no hope.

One cold December night, I would make an attempt to end my life. I planned on hanging myself. Fortunately, I backed out at the last second. I began to hate myself. The court ordered that my father be granted supervised *"therapeutic"* visitation. However, nothing about it was therapeutic. It was there that I would be told by my father that I was the reason for my parents' divorce.

During this period in my life, I would be granted a wish by the *Make- A-Wish Foundation*. All that was required was for both parents to sign a permission slip stating that I may be granted a wish. My mother gladly signed. My father, however, would refuse to sign. He said that I did not deserve to be granted a wish, as I wasn't sick enough, and I needed to let someone sicker have a trip instead of me. I would have to wait until I turned 18 to sign off for myself.

The depression would follow me into high school, where I was constantly in the guidance counselor's office, not because I wanted to be, but because they told me I missed too much school and there was too much missed work. The school didn't know the extent of my mental state until one day, a visiting social worker came in and asked me how I was. I responded by saying, *"I wanna kill myself"*.

The school contacted my mother and let her know what was going on.

I would miss school often due to my poor mental health. It was so bad that I had to repeat the 9th grade. I was transferred to a school for kids with mental health issues. I didn't learn like the other kids. In math, I would often find alternative solutions to equations. But because NYS believes in Common Core Math, if I had the right answer, I would still be marked wrong.

I wouldn't solve it like the curriculum taught. Nothing seemed to fit my learning style. The director of Special Education called my mom and suggested homeschooling. I would eventually try homeschooling and would work on getting my GED.

In 2021, I considered myself a high school dropout. But during this time, I began my healing journey through therapy. I have been in therapy since late 2017. But I didn't really start taking it seriously until the pandemic started.

In 2022, I was finally 18 and was able to sign off on my wish. My wish was to go to Disney World and stay in the now-

closed Star Wars Galactic Star Cruiser. On top of that, I was able to go to the beach and see the Atlantic Ocean for the first time. And I would also visit Epcot Center. I felt happier than I'd have ever been. I came out of my shell. I wasn't the quiet, shy kid who sheltered himself. I wasn't tired, and I didn't have a migraine. I felt alive for the first time.

Through hard work and a lot of tears shed, I started to heal. I would begin to love myself for who I was. Scars and all. I wore my scars like a badge of honor and would nickname myself *"The Warrior"*. I still have my bad days; however, I've come far from where I began. I started helping others with their trauma. I finally felt like I wasn't alone. No matter what I may go through, I have an army cheering me on.

Even on my darkest days, I look back and see how much I went through. And how I conquered my hardships. That no matter what happens, I can do it. I am a warrior. I am Mike Xander. I will win.

This chapter is dedicated to my dear friend Leonard Michael Castrianno, who sadly perished in the 9/11 attacks. He worked for Cantor Fitzgerald in the Twin Towers.

Without him, this story would never be possible. I know for a fact that he watches over us every day. Michael was named after Leonard; they both have so many of the best qualities. I miss him every day!

"Every time my heart beats is an act of defiance to all those who have ever doubted me. I'm still here because I am a warrior."-
Mike Xander

HEATHER AND MICHAEL "XANDER" COTTOM

Heather and Michael Cottom are a passionate and inspiring duo dedicated to encouraging others to pursue their dreams and live with purpose.

Heather is an aspiring writer who is building a vibrant, supportive community for readers, writers, and dreamers alike. Through her journey, she aims to create a space filled with inspiration, connection, and encouragement, inviting others to step boldly into their own creative paths.

Michael is known for his kind, generous, and compassionate spirit. With a heart for helping others, he aspires to become a counselor for children with special needs, using his own life experiences to offer understanding, support, and guidance to those who need it most.

Together, Heather and Mike embody resilience, mutual support, and a shared commitment to uplifting others, reminding people that with encouragement, compassion, and belief, anything is possible.

Connect with Heather and Mike

FB: hmdny11989 & mike.xander.931796

STORY OF FA'APEPELE HUNKIN

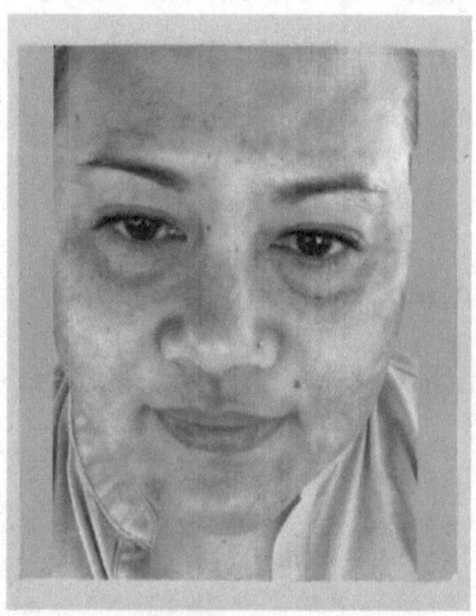

STILL STANDING, STILL LOVING, STILL SERVING

There was a time when I did not recognize the woman staring back at me in the mirror. Her eyes were tired, her smile was guarded, and her spirit was bruised from years of carrying pain she never learned how to release. She looked strong on the outside, capable and composed, but inside she was unraveling quietly, layer by layer, under the weight of profound grief, trauma, responsibility, and survival.

That woman was me.

In September 2018, I was broken, lost, and exhausted in ways I did not yet have words for. I was functioning, leading, loving, and serving, but I was not healing. And I was an alcoholic.

My unraveling did not happen overnight. It happened slowly and silently, disguised as coping. I knew how to be strong for everyone else, how to show up, how to love deeply, and how to serve faithfully, but I did not know how to tend to my own wounds. I mean, I was pouring so much to someone who can't even hand me back a cup.

I did not know how to sit with pain without trying to numb it. Alcohol became my escape. My quiet companion. My way of softening grief I had never processed and trauma I had never named. I told myself I was managing. I told myself I was in control. But deep down, I knew I was drowning while smiling for the world. Even then, even in my brokenness, God had not left me.

The turning point came on December 28, 2021, after a doctor's appointment that changed the course of my life. I was told my cholesterol level was 456, a number so high it could no longer be ignored. My body was speaking loudly after years of being silenced. In that moment, I stood at a crossroads, continuing to numb the pain or finally choosing life. That day, I chose life.

In that moment, choosing life meant more than quitting alcohol. I chose love, and I chose myself. It meant choosing honesty over denial and faith over fear. I realized that if I did not change, my body would eventually choose for me. I felt scared, exposed, and uncertain, yet deeply aware that God was giving me another chance.

I prayed quietly, asking God to guide me through what I did not yet know how to do. I did not have a perfect plan, but I had a willing heart. That day marked the beginning of learning how to care for myself with love, intention, grace, and accountability.

For the first time, I truly believed my life was worth protecting, not just for others, but for me. I chose to give up alcohol, not out of fear, but out of love for the life God had already preserved. Sobriety became obedience. It became stewardship. It became faith in motion. I walked out of that appointment knowing healing would require honesty, discipline, gratitude, surrender, and self-love.

That decision reignited my **FLY**, First Love Yourself, journey. **FLY** became my declaration that loving myself was not selfish; it was sacred. It taught me how to honor my body, protect my peace, and nurture my spirit. Healing stopped being an idea and became a daily practice. Every sober day became an act of worship. Every healthy choice became a prayer in motion.

Today, I am four years sober on my **FLY** journey. Four years of choosing clarity over chaos. Four years of choosing discipline over distraction. Four years of choosing myself because God chose me first.

By January 2026, my cholesterol level dropped to 155. That number represents far more than physical improvement. It represents consistency, surrender, faith, and grace. What once measured my decline now stands as evidence of God's restoring power, inside and out. But the journey did not stop there.

In 2023, my life was tested in ways I could never have imagined. I survived a heart attack that required a one-stent placement due to an eighty percent blockage.

In 2024, I survived three strokes, each one threatening to end my story. The second stroke revealed a blockage on the right side of my neck and caused muscle impairment that made chewing and daily tasks difficult. I also experienced internal bleeding that nearly took my life. The third stroke uncovered a three-point-five-millimeter blockage in my brain. Doctors later discovered seven nodules in my left breast, adding yet another layer of fear and uncertainty. By every medical standard, I should not be here. But God said otherwise.

In the quiet moments after survival, I learned that healing is not instant and it is not linear. There were days I grieved the version of myself I once knew, and days I feared the uncertainty of who I was becoming. I wrestled with patience, with surrender, and with learning how to rest without guilt. God met me in those moments, reminding me that slowing down was not failure, it was wisdom. Each pause became an invitation to trust Him more deeply. I learned that survival carries responsibility, not to rush forward, but to honor the life that was preserved. God was not only restoring my body, but He was also reshaping my heart, my priorities, and my purpose.

There were days my body felt fragile and my future uncertain. Days fear whispered that I had survived so much only to lose the battle anyway. Yet even then, especially then, God's grace carried me. When my strength failed, His did not. When my confidence wavered, His promises stood firm.

There were days my heart ached in ways words could barely hold. Days when I could not wash myself, clothe myself, or even brush my teeth without effort. Days when my legs would not cooperate, and I had to crawl the thirteen steps of my home just to reach upstairs, then rely on a walker to make it to my room.

Battling memory loss after multiple strokes was frightening and frustrating, and some days felt heavier than others. But even in those moments, I made a decision. I would not give up. Quitting has never been an option for me. Every crawl was an act of faith. Every step was an act of love. Every attempt to remember was an act of hope.

God was rebuilding me slowly, intentionally, and with purpose, strengthening not just my body, but my spirit, and reminding me that I carry the HEART OF A WARRIOR.

Today, I am blessed to testify that I no longer have any blockages in my body. No heart blockages. No brain blockages. No neck blockages. Only grace.

Miracles do not always arrive loudly. Sometimes they come through sustained healing, daily obedience, and unwavering faith. God did not just save my life. He restored it.

At the heart of my healing journey are my children, my granddaughter, and my fur baby, my living why. I am deeply grateful for each of them, especially my son, Dean Jr., who lovingly cares for me when my daughters are at work. His patience, strength, and presence have been a gift I will never take lightly. My granddaughter, Princess Milan, is joy wrapped in purpose. Her laughter reminds me daily why choosing life mattered. And my fur baby, Deabo, who is with me around the clock, has been my constant companion, offering comfort, calm, and unconditional love throughout my recovery. I truly do not know where I would be without them.

I am also forever grateful to my family and friends whose prayers, love, and unwavering support carried me through the hardest seasons. Every breakthrough I experienced was not walked alone. It was covered in prayer and surrounded by love.

Sharing my story became part of my healing. On days I felt weak, encouraging someone else gave me strength. On days my body needed rest, my testimony still carried purpose. God showed me that my pain was never meant to be hidden. It was meant to be healed out loud.

My transformation is not simply from addiction to sobriety. It is from brokenness to wholeness, from survival to service, from grief to grace, and from asking why me to declaring, use me.

Today, when I look in the mirror, I see a Warrior Woman refined by grace. A Samoan Warrior Woman who understands that being still here is not accidental, it is intentional. I am still here by God's grace. And because I am still here, I live differently. I love deeper. I serve harder. My scars no longer define my pain. They reveal the story of how I survived and healed.

I am deeply grateful for the woman I was yesterday, because she introduced me to the Warrior Woman I am today. Every version of me survived something so the next version could rise stronger. I honor her courage, her endurance, and her faith for carrying me through seasons I did not think I would survive. I inspire you to be grateful for your yesterdays, too, because they are not failures; they are foundations. Who you were helped shape who you are becoming.

If you are reading this and feel lost, tired, or ashamed of where you have been, hear me clearly. Your story is not over. Your pain is not your identity. Your heart still beats because your life still has purpose.

Transformation and healing begin the moment you tell the truth and trust God with the rest. Brokenness does not get the final word. Grace does.

I am still standing. Still loving. Still serving. By God's grace. I am not my diagnosis.

Remember always, YOU MATTER. Keep on keeping on, one love, one step, one prayer, one heartbeat at a time, with the HEART OF A WARRIOR.

FA'APEPELE HUNKIN

Fa'apepele Hunkin is a proud Samoan Warrior Woman, mother of five, grandmother to Princess Milan, dog Mama to fur baby Deabo, and retired U.S. Army Combat Veteran whose life embodies love, grace, faith, and resilience.

She is a 20x bestselling author, transformational speaker, and a heart and three-stroke survivor whose journey reflects the power of God's mercy and divine purpose. She is a survivor of divorce, alcohol addiction, and near-death battles that tested every ounce of her faith; Through it all, she stands as living proof that God's grace is greater than any diagnosis. With every breath, she declares, *"I made it by grace, not chance, and I AM NOT MY DIAGNOSIS."*

Pele is the author of HEART OF A WARRIOR: The Humble Journey of a Samoan Warrior, Gracefully Growing Through

Grief with the HEART OF A WARRIOR: A 30-Day Journal of Healing, Reflection, Love and Hope, and Color My Comeback Coloring Book from Battlefields to Prayerfields.

She has co-authored seventeen bestselling anthologies and describes her transformation as "From Battlefield to Prayerfield of Becoming HER: Healed, Empowered, Resilient." As founder of Pele Inspire~Embracing Authentic Love and visionary creator of the FLY~First Love Yourself Movement, Pele empowers women, veterans, warriors, and youth to heal, rise, and walk boldly in their God-given purpose.

Her message is simple yet profound: When you FLY-First Love Yourself, you can rise gracefully and unapologetically through anything.

Through her work, she reminds the world that we all carry the HEART OF A WARRIOR and can PELE: Persevere Enough Love Everywhere.

Connect with Pele

Website: www.peleinspire.com
Email: pelehunkino3@gmail.com
FB: www.facebook.com/peleinspire
FB: www.facebook.com/pelehunkin
IG: www.instagram.com/peleinspire

THE STORY OF HEATHER DURHAM–BELT

AT THE BEGINNING OF MY JOURNEY, I BELIEVED THE SCALE HELD THE ANSWER TO MY HEALTH.

I remember those early days vividly. Looking back now, I can see how much I was carrying…emotionally, physically, and spiritually…long before I understood what it was doing to my body. During my marriage to my first husband, I often carried the emotional and practical weight of our household. He was a great provider, and I'm grateful that his work allowed me to be home with our five children and homeschool them, but much of the day-to-day responsibility rested on my shoulders. I wasn't sleeping enough. The house was always busy, full of activity and noise, and I felt like I was constantly running on empty. My body was silently keeping score. At the time, I assumed it was personal failure. Now I understand it was physiology…my body responding exactly the way a body under prolonged pressure does.

After 17 years of marriage, I received divorce papers, and my life shifted again. I went back to nursing school as a single momma in my 40s with five kids and juggling parenting. Even though I was remarried during my last year of nursing school… much of the day-to-day of parenting fell on me. Managing work, home, children, appointments (after a motor vehicle accident that totaled the car), and my children's school activities left me drained… but I managed to survive, graduate nursing school, and pass my boards the FIRST time. Within a few months, I began working night shift full-time. The stress of managing a home, sleeping 4-5 hours on the days I worked, being a wife and mom to my kids, was exhausting, and yet I survived… BUT GOD.

Looking back, the final eight weeks of nursing school were relentless and exhausting on a whole new level. I barely slept. My brain was on constant overdrive, running through lectures, clinical, homework, maintaining my home, and all of the family logistics. My body reacted in some very dramatic ways. I gained 40 pounds in just two months… without changing anything… At the time, I didn't understand what was happening. I just remember looking in the mirror and feeling confused, discouraged, and wondering if my body had somehow turned against me. I was walking several days a week and eating reasonably healthy, but it wasn't enough. I quickly began to see my hormones were imbalanced, my cortisol was high, and exhaustion weighed down every part of my being. I felt it physically… in my muscles, in my mind, and in my spirit. My body was sensitive to stress and sleep deprivation, and it was showing me… in no uncertain terms… that I wasn't taking care of myself well. That concentrated period of weight gain was a wake-up call, one I didn't fully understand at the time, but it planted the first seed of awareness that would guide my health journey for years to come.

Even in that season, I wanted control. I thought if I could just lose the weight, hit the right numbers, drink enough water, and never indulge in any sort of unhealthy snack… I would be okay… BUT… I wasn't. Looking back, I can see the real transformation would require far more than that… it would require faith, curiosity, intentionality, and learning to truly listen to my body.

At the end of 2018, my cousin reached out to me about a program that would help me lose weight… little did I know it would be an answer to so much more than the number on the scale. The program helped me take off the weight... BUT... it really helped me transform and shape the way I think about health... so much that I knew, as an RN, I wanted to coach the program I had used to serve others and bridge the gap between my patients in the hospital and what their Drs wanted them to do. People needed to learn that it isn't about a list of dos and don'ts, but about creating the life you want... about being around for your grand-babies, your friends, and loved ones... being able to run, jump, crawl on the floor with those precious little ones versus sit on the couch and recliner watching life pass them by. After nine months of coaching in the white spaces of my day... I was able to buy back my time from nursing by persistently sharing with people and letting them know they didn't have to stay stuck... and to add additional accountability to my own health journey.

After several years of maintaining my weight loss and transforming on the outside... 60 pounds in six months, improving my triglycerides by 139 points, increasing my HDL(good cholesterol) by 18 points, and keeping my weight off for four years... everything shifted. Mold exposure changed my health dramatically. I began gaining weight despite doing all the *"right"* things... eating healthy, exercising, resting, and managing stress as best as I could. Fatigue worsened. Thyroid nodules appeared and kept growing. I felt disoriented, frustrated, and honestly, afraid.

In that season, I had to become my own advocate. I didn't have a functional medicine doctor in my area who could guide me, so I dove into research... YouTube videos with Functional Drs, blogs, articles, and online communities became my teachers. My daughter's knowledge and experience with mold exposure helped me recognize the problem in my current home and most likely the home before the one I currently live in. I paid for functional lab work, and the results confirmed what I suspected... Chronic Inflammatory Response Syndrome (CIRS).

Emotionally, it was heavy but a relief at the same time... I didn't feel crazy... even though my body felt like a stranger, my confidence shaken. I questioned my ability to coach others when I couldn't keep my own health on track...but even in this season of uncertainty, God's presence was steadily guiding me. I began to see this season not as a punishment or failure, but as an opportunity for growth. He had walked me through every previous season, equipping me to serve others more deeply, and this challenge, too, I did not want to waste... I wanted it to have purpose.

The turning point came through SURRENDER. On a Wellness Integrated Now (WIN) call, I learned the difference between a *"diet"* mindset and a ***"health"*** mindset. A *"diet"* focuses on numbers, restrictions, and perfection. A ***"health"*** mindset nurtures the body to the best of its ability, focusing on sustainable habits and overall well-being rather than the scale.

This shifted everything. I realized that true health isn't about perfection. It's about faithfulness, curiosity, and care. It's about listening to your body, leaning into community, my coach, the system, and trusting God. Isaiah 46:10 reminds me that He knows the end from the beginning. My experiences from high-risk pregnancies, a divorce I did not want, mold exposure, thyroid issues, and life's demands… have always been a part of a bigger plan.

I began taking intentional steps rooted in this mindset: surrendering control, experimenting thoughtfully with new tools, and focusing on holistic health on a deeper level. I shifted my attention from weight to vitality, energy, inflammation, mindset, and sustainable habits for this season. Transformation was no longer about the number on the scale, or a sprint: it was about doing the heart work, the hardest work… and it was a marathon.

Healing continues through small, consistent choices… quiet, daily, often unglamorous actions. I focus on sleep, giving myself permission for power naps when my body needs them. Walking five days a week. Trying to do strength training 2-3 times a week. I monitor blood work, track inflammatory markers, and research new ways to support my body functionally.

I pay attention to my blood sugar, protein intake, and inflammatory foods. I avoid things my body reacts to… egg whites, casein, peanuts, soy, corn, wheat, coffee, and cacao… the last two I struggle with… especially the coffee… I am trying to learn to love detox and green tea… LOL. I try to read labels carefully, take supplements, hydrate, and move my body thoughtfully, adjusting exercises as needed based on how I am feeling and my energy levels.

Curiosity drives me. I encouraged my cousin, a very knowledgeable and experienced Nurse Practitioner, to explore integrative functional health, joking that I'd be her guinea pig if she ever needed one. Together, we have shared and tried new strategies, new supplements, new technologies, and wellness tools… things that support my immune system, reduce inflammation, create energy, and overall vitality. Some days, the changes are subtle. Other days, they are profound. Each small shift reminds me that consistent curiosity and action create momentum.

Challenges remain. Fatigue, a full schedule, running a Health and Wellness coaching practice, and ongoing responsibilities make some days more exhausting and heavier than others. But now, I celebrate progress wherever I see it. I remind myself that my body is like a delicate houseplant, needing water, sunlight, gentle movement, and protection from excess stress. I intentionally release what doesn't serve me and respond differently to what I cannot control. I fight the temptation to see myself as a victim, choosing instead to be a victor… living with the perspective that life happens FOR me, not to me.

I am not alone. My faith keeps me grounded. My husband and children support me when I need rest. My children help without complaint. My friends understand, and my Healthy community reminds me I'm not walking this path alone. Even my clients encourage me through honesty and shared experiences.

Looking back, exhausted, stressed, and frustrated with my body, I see how far I've come. True transformation is about more than weight or perfection… It's about curiosity, faithfulness, and consistent action.

The choices I make every day… sleeping enough, moving my body regularly, fueling my body well, exploring new strategies, new tools and supplements, leaning on faith and my Healthy community. Shape how I feel, think, and live. Transformation isn't about reaching a destination… It's about showing up intentionally every day.

Maybe parts of my story feel familiar to you.

Maybe you've tried to do all the "right" things and still felt like your body was working against you. Maybe you've wondered if something deeper was going on.

If that's you, I want you to know this: your story isn't over.

I haven't arrived. I'm still learning. I'm still healing. But if my story shows anything, it's this: transformation doesn't begin when life becomes easy. It begins the moment we decide to stay curious, stay faithful, and take the next step forward.

I hope by sharing my story… the struggles, new tools, strategies, and ongoing work… You can see that transformation is possible for you. There's a path forward, and it begins with paying attention, being willing to learn, and staying committed to caring for yourself in ways that honor your body, mind, and spirit.

Transformation doesn't start when life gets easier… it starts when we choose to keep showing up.

If parts of my story feel familiar, I want you to know there is hope and there is a path forward. None of us are meant to navigate these journeys alone, and I am grateful for every opportunity to walk alongside others who are learning to live healthier, fuller lives.

HEATHER DURHAM-BELT

Heather Belt is a nurse, transformational lifestyle coach, business mentor, and mom of five who is passionate about helping others create lasting change from the inside out. Like many women, Heather once believed that health was defined by a number on the scale. Through her own journey, she discovered that true wellness goes far beyond weight—it involves mindset, stress, habits, faith, and learning how to care for the body as a whole.

With a background in nursing and more than seven years of coaching experience, Heather has helped over 600 people directly and indirectly pursue healthier, more purposeful lives. Her approach focuses on whole-person transformation—supporting people in building healthier habits for their body, renewing their mindset, and creating greater stability in their lives so stress no longer controls their health.

In addition to guiding individuals on their health journeys, Heather also mentors coaches and wellness entrepreneurs who want to build purpose-driven health and wellness businesses so they can create greater impact while helping others live healthier lives.

Heather believes true transformation happens when people begin caring for their body, renewing their mind, and building lives aligned with their faith and purpose.

Heather lives in Southern Indiana with her family and loves building meaningful connections, encouraging others, and walking alongside people on their journey toward health and transformation.

Connect with Heather

Email: connect.heatherbelt@gmail.com

FB: Heather Durham-Belt

IG: @heather_belt7

THE STORY OF TWEE SHAW

THE FIRE THAT FORCED ME TO STAY

The Day the World Split

The world did not warn me it was about to divide my life in two.

One moment, I was driving along an ordinary stretch of highway, my son, Maximus, in the back seat, guarding a birthday cake stacked dangerously high with strawberries and chocolate. He held the box carefully with both hands, studying it the way he studies a chessboard now, already thinking about how to keep everything balanced.

He and my mum turned her kitchen into something that would have unsettled her on any other day. She liked order, clear surfaces, and everything in its place, but not this morning. Bowls were left where they landed. Flour dusted the bench and floor. Sticky fingerprints marked cupboard doors. She didn't stop him when he measured badly, poured too much, or insisted on his own combinations and additions. She simply sang with him.

My mum loved to feed people. Her kitchen was never just for meals. It was where she could create from whatever was there. When complimented, she always answered the same, *"The secret ingredient is love"*. Mum worked by feel, trusting what seemed right rather than anything measured, and that morning she let him do the same.

At one point, without telling her, Maximus slipped popping candy into the mix and motioned for me to keep his secret. Later, he told me it reminded him of her, the way it crackled and sparked unexpectedly. Small, but alive in a way that changed everything like magic.

Now sitting behind me in the car, holding the cake box protectively, Maximus started singing: *"Give me a home among the gum trees..."*

He leaned forward so I could see him in the mirror, *"Mum, sing with me, please?"*

I glanced at him. His eyes were bright, his hands steady. I opened my mouth to answer, but my attention had already shifted.

The Victims of Crime process.

The wording felt wrong in my body. It asked for a version of the story I had never allowed to fully exist. To bring it forward, name it and allow it to be examined. The weight of it landed before I could think it through. It settled heavy and low, pressing through my chest and stomach. Not sharp, just present. The kind of pressure that doesn't lift easily.

The word victim didn't fit.

It asked for an admission I had never made, even to myself. That I had been powerless and could not stop what had been done to me. My body rejected it before my mind could form it.

Staying inside anything long enough for it to land had never felt safe. I had learned early to move, to leave, and to keep going before anything could close in, but this asked for the opposite.

It required stillness and presence that my body responded to with tightness, narrowed breath, and discomfort. My body craved an entirely different place where nothing needed to be explained or proven. The misalignment settled deeper as the feelings hovered unresolved, unable to find any suitable place to land.

The tyres scraped against the white line with a sharp, dragging sound, and I turned the wheel too quickly, correcting harder than I needed to.

"Mum, watch out."

"I've got it!"

My words came automatically and practiced. To convince him as much as myself.

But something had already shifted.

The connection between the moment and my body loosened. The familiar low buzzing began, like a swarm of bees waking beneath my ribs. It didn't ease the tension; it built through it. The sensation rose through my chest, an internal lift I had known since childhood, the quiet signal that came just before separation from my body and whatever was about to happen.

The vibration intensified.

I watched the scene continue without me. My body remained in the driver's seat, hands on the wheel, but I was no longer inside it. Below, my body slumped forward against the steering wheel. The car moved ahead, but no longer held its line. It drifted left across the edge of the highway and onto a dirt track that cut down the slope beside it.

From that height, everything appeared without sound and seemed unnaturally calm.

The change wasn't happening outside of. It came the way it always had, a loosening from the inside. Not sudden enough to resist or strong enough to stop. Just enough to separate.

I was watching without sound or sense; I was the one inside it. Sometimes the mind leaves the body before the body understands why.

The road did not disappear, but I did.

Some memories do not fade. They wait until they can be seen.

The Leaving

The road disappeared.

Not gradually. One moment it was there, and then it wasn't, replaced by something older, something my body recognised before my mind could catch up.

A small boat packed tight, holding more people than it should have. Bodies pressed tightly together, legs against legs, shoulders against strangers. There was no space between us, only the weight of each other shifting with the movement beneath.

Time stretched across a month at sea until the days stopped separating. The sun sat on us without moving. It burned through the top of my head, down into my shoulders, and back. Skin tightened, then split and peeled. Salt settled into it and stayed there. There was no shade, no relief, only the slow shift in space after bodies were swallowed by the ocean.

I was pressed into my mum, wrapped around her, my arms locked in place as if letting go would mean losing her entirely. Her body leaned heavily against me, unable to hold herself upright anymore. I carried her without choice, adjusting with each movement of the boat to keep her from slipping further.

It started in me first.

Not as something I chose. A shift I could feel before I understood it. The edges of things softened so the heat, the pressure, and the hunger did not land with the same force. I noticed the way people dimmed more each day until there was less sound, less movement, less hope. Faces lost their expression, and the light in the eyes started to go out, too.

At some point, the tone on the boat changed. I didn't need to understand every word because my body didn't require language to translate. My mother's unresponsiveness had marked her. I was a malnourished child with no strength to lift her or make her seem lighter than she was. I simply held her, adjusting with each shift of the boat, trying to keep her upright until hunger overrode all logic. My body stopped waiting to be fed and sought sustenance from my mother, but when it didn't come, I bit angrily against skin that had already given more than it had.

The taste changed, turned metallic in my mouth. There was almost nothing there, barely a trace of blood. Her body had already given me everything it could. I saw a tiny red mark on her shirt that didn't spread. It should have stopped me straight away, but my body begged for more. My mother stayed where she was, her weight leaning heavily into me. She had nothing left to give.

Something in me shifted then.

Not outwardly. Not in a way anyone could see. But inside, where the pressure eased just enough to keep holding her without breaking. The heat, the weight, the voices were still there, but they no longer landed the same way.

I didn't leave her by choice or thought, but for survival – to leave the hunger and the pain. My grip on her didn't loosen, but the rest of me left until the distance from the boat dulled enough of the edges for me, the heat, the fear, and the pain to stop landing the same way.

That distance did not stay on the boat.

It followed me into places that were meant to be safer and never were. Bedrooms with doors that closed and air that changed. I knew before anything happened. Not as a thought, just a shift in my body that knew first.

The lift would come. The buzzing would follow, low at first, then filling everything until there was no space left for anything else. My body stayed where it was, but I ejected. Pressure without weight. Movement without meaning. Even when my body bled, it did not register the way it should have. I could see it, but it stayed separate from me, something happening to a body I was no longer fully inside.

Other times, I left to protect my mother. My guilt of biting her on that boat stayed with me, sharp and unrelenting, binding me to protecting her in the same way she had given herself for me. I came to believe that if I spoke about what was being done to me, it would harm her, or she would think I was lying, so I kept it in and stepped out of myself instead.

That was where the pattern refined itself. Not in one moment, but in repetition. Each time the pressure built and there was no way to move, no way to speak, no one to step in, the same separation opened inside the body where my body would remain, but I would not. There was no decision in it, and it would arrive the same way each time.

The ceiling would come into focus before I even realised I was looking at it. I would count patterns on bedspreads, threads in the carpet, anything fixed enough to hold while the rest of the room dropped away.

Later, it appeared in places that did not carry the same danger but drew the same response from my body. A stretch of road. The sense of pressure building without a clear source. My body would shift before I understood why.

Doctors prescribed a smorgasbord of medication to help me sleep, to help me function, but all it did was flatten everything further. It dulled the edges but took something else with it. I moved through days without urgency, without the signals that would have told me to stop.

At one point, I found myself on a highway with no clear memory of how I had entered it, my body still carrying on as though nothing had been interrupted while cars and log trucks swerved to miss me, and people shouted from their windows as they drove past. I felt no panic in the moment, only distance.

What broke this episode was not fear for myself, but a phone call I couldn't hear – just a knowledge someone was calling. The thought that someone needed me cut through everything else, and the distance collapsed all at once. The sudden roar of trucks rushed in. Wind whipped my hair into my mouth and my eyes. Tarmac burned against my bare feet. The realisation that someone cared enough to check on me shifted something I had not known how to reach. It made me say out loud, finally, that I needed help.

That help arrived in the form of three life-changing days in Sydney, at a Brandon Bays course, sitting inside my body longer than felt safe and allowing things to surface without leaving them. It did not remove the pattern, but it changed my relationship to it. The distance no longer arrived without being noticed.

And now, in the car, with the road no longer where it should be and the ground falling away beneath us, it moved through me again with that same familiarity.

What once kept me alive was the act of leaving

Fragments in Red Light

There is no memory of the impact.

The car striking the tree exists only as a gap in the sequence, a place where something should be but isn't. What follows does not arrange itself into a timeline. It arrives in fragments, each piece detached from the next, resisting any attempt to place it in order.

Red appears first. Not attached to an object or contained within a shape, just colour pressing inward without edges, carrying the sense of something that has already happened but will not show itself fully.

Then movement. Not initiated by me, not something I can trace back to a beginning. My body is already being carried or repositioned, already in transit, without any awareness of how it started or who is moving me.

Another memory surfaces without warning.

Land after a month at sea. Hands pulling me out of the boat, away from my unconscious mother, while I reach back for her, my arms extending toward something already out of reach. My mouth opens, but no sound comes. The dryness is complete, sealing everything inside. That separation settled somewhere deeper than memory and never fully left.

Then the distance changes.

It is no longer between a child and her mother. It is between my son and me.

At first, his voice reaches me faintly, as though it has travelled a great distance before finding me. I try to follow it back, pulling my attention toward wherever my body must still be, resisting the familiar lifting sensation that has already begun to take hold.

The hillside sharpens briefly into focus beneath me.

Not from inside the car. From above it.

The car is already crumpled against the tree on the slope, the trunk holding it in place, stopping it from sliding further down the embankment, where it might have disappeared from the highway above. There is no memory of how it got there, only that it is already there. Then his voice again. *"Mum!"*

This time, it carries breath and urgency rather than the hollow quality of something remembered. I hold onto it as something physical, a thread I can follow back to the moment before I leave.

After that, the sequence fractures again.

Voices move around me, but do not match the movement of mouths. Sound and image have slipped out of alignment. I keep forcing my attention toward Maximus, using the sound of him as an anchor while the world glitches in and out of focus. Smoke begins to thread upward from the front of the car, thin at first, then darker as it curls around the bark. The slope falls sharply away beneath it, loose earth, scrub, a hollow where the wreck could easily have vanished from sight.

The scene widens again without warning, and I am already above it, looking down through the same fractured separation that has taken me before. I see Tonia running across the gravel toward the ambulance and the fire truck I never heard arrive. The red of it stands stark against the pale sky while smoke and flames begin to climb the trunk of the tree below. A moment later, I see Tonia reach Maximus. His small body shakes as she pulls him into her arms.

A thought moves through me, quiet and detached. I wonder if I am dead?

For a moment, the entire scene seems suspended in silence beneath me. Flames move further up the trunk, orange and restless against the bark, sending thick ribbons of black into the air. Everything continues, but the sound does not reach me.

Another thought slips through. If the unexpected interstate visitors had not arrived unannounced, my mother would have been in the car with us that day. I wonder whether the additional weight would have changed what the tree could hold, or whether gravity would have taken us all.

Then the image breaks again.

When awareness returns, I am inside another car with the door open. Air moves in from outside, and my eyes adjust enough to make out a man in the front seat speaking steadily. I see his mouth moving, but struggle to make sense of his words. His presence feels calm, containing rather than demanding. Later, I learn he is a firefighter who witnessed the crash.

Beside the open door, a woman leans toward me, watching my face carefully.

My thirst arrives suddenly. The burn in my throat feels ancient, the dryness not belonging only to this moment. I motion weakly for water, but she shakes her head and says something about surgery.

The dryness pulls something else with it. Salt, heat, and an overcrowded boat. The body remembering before the mind has a chance to separate it. The lifting sensation returns.

I search for Maximus and bear down against the lift.

Then the scene shifts again without explanation.

White interior panels. Equipment secured neatly along the walls. The steady vibration of an engine travelling through the stretcher beneath my body. I am inside an ambulance. The transition feels less like movement and more like missing time, as though entire pieces of it have been removed between one breath and the next. Voices drift in and out of reach, as though spoken underwater or from behind something I cannot move through.

My body feels close, but not fully mine yet. Sensation returns in fragments, then thins again. Stiffness pulls along my spine. Smoke still clings faintly to my clothes beneath the antiseptic.

Then panic cuts through everything.

Maximus.

I try to move, instinctively searching for him, but the brace around my neck holds me firmly in place. My chest buzzes furiously, as if the hive inside me has been attacked. A face leans into view and says gently, *"We've got you."*

The words land, but they do not answer the only question that matters.

Then I hear him.

Not distant. Not fading. Right here.

It cuts through everything else, through the red, through the silence, through the distance I had already begun to disappear into. My body responds before thought can catch up. Something inside me tightens and drops fast, dragging me back down into myself. The separation collapses without warning. One moment I am above it, the next I am inside it again.

Breath returns hard and uneven. Pain follows, immediate and unmistakable, spreading through muscle and bone as everything comes back online at once.

I do not leave. The movement continues around me. Hands adjust, lift, reposition. Ceiling panels pass overhead in sharp white blocks that no longer fracture or disappear. Sound returns in partial layers, enough to confirm the world is holding its shape again.

I search for him without turning my head, my body scanning for where he is, for whether the distance has opened again.

Then I see him briefly. Chocolate and strawberries streaked across his shirt. The red mark of the seatbelt across his chest was otherwise untouched. He speaks about how tasty the cake was and his disappointment that no one else got to try it. That detail undoes me. In the middle of smoke, fire, and strangers running towards us, my son's greatest regret is that the birthday cake he had guarded so carefully had been eaten by accident.

His body suddenly folds forward without warning. The shock he has been holding releases all at once. He is guided away almost immediately, not abruptly, but with the quiet efficiency of people who know exactly where to move him. Doors close between us. The distance returns, this time measured in walls and corridors I cannot cross.

I lie still. The brace, holding my neck in place. Sensation continues to return layer by layer as the adrenaline drains and leaves everything exposed. Pain deepens, spreading wider as it settles.

Underneath it, something older surfaces. Exhaustion. The kind that has lived quietly in the body for years. The slow accumulation of strain, of holding, of enduring.

Machines take over where my body cannot. X-rays. Scans. Cold surfaces. Instructions that blur as I am moved again and again. The sound that once lived inside my chest now exists outside of me, carried by monitors tracking each breath and heartbeat.

The body holds its own record and doesn't organise itself into a story or sequence. Fear, separation, and endurance settle into muscle and tissue, shaping what remains long after the moment has passed.

For most of my life, when intensity reached a certain point, something in me stepped away. The lifting sensation would come, and I would leave before the moment could fully land.

The pull to leave keeps appearing, but it did not complete. Not while he needed me, I would not shift. Because when everything else fractures, Maximus is what remains.

The Voice Before Impact

Maximus told me my father had come to him. Not in the ambulance or hospital, but before any of it. He said he saw him outside the window, moving beside the car. He recognised him immediately. The moustache, the smile, and his message:

"Don't worry. Everything will be OK."

My father used that sentence often, and it always felt too blasé for what I was facing, so I resisted it. Hearing it again through Maximus did not feel simple. It stayed, as though it had been waiting for a moment, I could not argue with.

The day held a strange coherence. Visitors from Melbourne who kept my mother at home. The dirt track without a barrier. The single tree halfway down the slope. A firefighter who happened to be passing. A nurse who came to help.

Maximus spoke about it with certainty. In his mind, his Poppy had been there from the beginning, guiding the car toward the only place that would hold it.

I did not argue with him.

My father had trusted what could be proven. Faith had never belonged to him, but near the end of his life, that certainty softened. My parents renewed their vows in Cana. Dad had told me his greatest fear was not dying but forgetting how much he loved her and loved us. But love remains where other things do not. His words stayed and finally landed.

The tree that stopped the car was a silver wattle, the kind that grows where ground has been disturbed, holding it long enough for other life to follow. It did not need to be large. It met the moment it was required to meet and was enough.

My father had loved trees. He spoke about returning to the earth, about becoming part of something that continued. He had been allergic to wattle, yet he would not cut it down. Dad's kindness filled a room. He sang loudly, hummed, and wore colours that refused to be ignored. My mother carried a different force. Where he grounded, she persisted. Her survival was driven by a refusal to disappear, even when everything around her gave way.

Between them, I had been raised by two forces, steadiness and fire, and Maximus carried both without effort.

What happened that day did not need to be proven. It held.

"Don't worry. Everything will be OK."

Before, survival had meant leaving.

The Pattern

My hands stayed on the wheel. I could feel the pressure of it, the exact place where my palms met the curve, the slight drag as the tyres tracked along the line of the highway.

The buzzing came first. Low at the start, a hum of bees waking beneath my ribs. It moved slowly until it spread, climbing higher, pressing behind my eyes, tightening across my chest. It always started this way and marked the point where my body would eject me from the moment before it could fully land.

Behind me, Maximus was still holding the cake he had built, the one he called *"The Leaning Tower of Love"*. The lid of the box could not close over it. It had been folded back from the start, the height of it too much, the angles too sharp, the layers stacked beyond what should have worked. Chocolate ganache softened beneath strawberries that slid with each small movement of the car. Chocolate-covered coffee beans pressed into the sides, the same ones my dad used to savour slowly, one at a time. Popping candy scattered through it like my mum's magic, hidden until it hit your tongue. Pillowy marshmallows, soft where everything else held firm. Sharp triangular shards of chocolate rose from the top like sails that should have snapped but didn't.

He had made it that way on purpose.

"Every bite needs to be a surprising explosion of love and flavour."

It was the kind of thing I had learned to tone down, to smooth out, to reduce before it became too much to manage.

He didn't.

Maximus held it as it was. It didn't matter that it took up more space than it should have. He had been unapologetic about it being too much of everything: texture, sweetness, crunch. He had built it past what should have been possible, and yet it was still standing.

Something in me recognised it.

I had told him it wouldn't fit.

"Don't worry," he said, already adjusting his grip on the box.

"Everything is going to be okay."

His words were familiar. I recognised them as my father's. The same ones I used to meet with quiet resistance, the reflex to push back against anything that did not come with proof.

This time I didn't.

They were the same words Maximus said before everything broke apart, not rushed or forced, just spoken in that same steady way, as if the outcome had already been decided.

Behind me, his hands moved with the weight. Each time the cake shifted, he adjusted, small, precise corrections, tilting the box just enough, steadying it before it could slip further. He wasn't thinking about it. He was already solving, not reacting.

The buzzing deepened. The surge followed quickly, my vision thinning at the edges, sound flattening. My body knew what came next. I was going to the same place I had gone when I had no voice, when no one stepped in, when leaving was the only way to stay intact.

Behind me, Maximus stayed with his cake, focusing more intensely as if anticipating the next shift. He didn't pull away as it became harder to hold.

I tightened my grip on the wheel. *"No!"*

The force pressed harder, the same pattern that had carried me through everything I had survived, every time I had set myself aside to keep something else from breaking.

But this time it met everything I had been built from. Every experience that had caused me to leave, every heartbreak, every injury, every fire, I should not have survived. They rose together.

"I am not leaving".

My hands tightened on the wheel. The buzzing did not disappear, but it changed. Each time it lifted, I pressed back into the seat beneath me, into the steady forward motion of the car. I focused on the line of the road, the vibration through the tyres, the feeling of my fingers gripping tighter than they needed to.

Then I heard him singing again.

"But when my mates all ask me

The place that I adore..."

I didn't need to hear the rest. My heart already knew that place was here.

That knowing changed the disconnection into something else. A warmth moved through the same places, slow and steady, settling where everything would usually split. I could still feel every crack. But instead of opening further, they began to hold.

For a long time, I had been the one holding things in place, adjusting, compensating, filling what was missing. Not chosen, just doing what was needed to keep the pieces together.

Now something felt different.

The pressure was still there, but it no longer felt like annihilation. It felt closer to what my father had carried, the way he held us without needing to announce it. Like the way Maximus held his cake, carefully adjusting as it leaned, steady, present, holding what he had made without apology.

The car continued forward. Trees flickered past in the periphery. Light shifted across the dashboard. Nothing outside of it changed. But inside, something landed.

The sound in my body shifted too, still dense, still present, but no longer something to escape. It thickened and slowed and held its shape instead of breaking apart.

The year Maximus turned five, he wanted a bee party. He spoke about bees as if everything about them mattered. The way they moved, the way they contributed, the way they kept everything going without being seen.

"Did you know honey never spoils?" he told me.

For most of my life, my body had known only one way to survive.

To leave.

But leaving had never been a decision. It was something my body did to keep me alive, a reflex that carried me away before pain could reach me. But somewhere between the fire, the red sirens, and the hospital lights, something changed. I felt the space open, but did not follow. Each time, I fought my way back. For him, for them, and for the part of me that still burned.

I stayed.

TWEE SHAW

*Certified ProCoach, Life Coach, and Master NLP Practitioner
and trauma-informed coach*

Twee Shaw is a certified ProCoach, Life Coach, Master NLP Practitioner, and trauma-informed coach dedicated to guiding individuals through healing, self-discovery, and personal transformation. Inspired by her name, meaning "water," her coaching philosophy is fluid, adaptable, and life-giving—meeting each client where they are while helping them move toward clarity and growth.

Drawing from her powerful lived experience as a Vietnamese refugee and survivor of childhood and domestic trauma, Twee brings deep empathy, authenticity, and understanding to her work. She creates safe, nurturing spaces where clients can explore their inner world, build resilience, and reconnect with their sense of self.

Using a holistic approach that blends NLP, somatic healing, and creative modalities such as art, music, and nature-based practices, Twee helps clients release limiting beliefs, regulate emotions, and develop practical strategies for lasting change. Her work is rooted in compassion and collaboration, empowering individuals to embrace self-love, strengthen their capacity for life's challenges, and step confidently into a more balanced, purposeful future.

Connect with Twee

https://zeniful.com.au/

FB: twee.shaw

RESOURCES AND HELPLINES

4ps Group LLC and Trunnis Goggins II
Connect with Trunnis Goggins II and find out how you can get involved in what he is doing, or if you are someone looking for help, reach out to the 4ps Group, and they can point you in the right direction.
https://4ps-group.com/

988 Suicide and Crisis Lifeline
At the 988 Suicide & Crisis Lifeline, we understand that life's challenges can sometimes be difficult. Whether you're facing mental health struggles, emotional distress, alcohol or drug use concerns, or just need someone to talk to, our caring counselors are here for you. You are not alone.
https://988lifeline.org/

American Cancer Society

The mission of the American Cancer Society is to improve the lives of people with cancer and their families through advocacy, research, and patient support, to ensure everyone has an opportunity to prevent, detect, treat, and survive cancer.
https://www.cancer.org/

HelpGuide

Any loss can cause grief, including the loss of a relationship, your health, your job, or a cherished dream. Learn how to better cope with what you're feeling and process your emotions in ways that allow you to heal.
https://www.helpguide.org/mental-health/grief

Minnesota Adult & Teen Challenge

Our mission is to assist men, women and teens in gaining freedom from chemical addictions and other life-controlling problems by addressing their physical, emotional and spiritual needs.
www.mntc.org

New Leaf New Life

Provides resources for overcoming addiction and re-entering society after incarceration.
https://newleafnewlife.org/
812-355-6842

The Sheila Smith Foundation

Mission: To redefine recovery, inspire hope, end stigma, and empower those in or seeking recovery from substance use,

mental health issues, trauma, and related life challenges to increase their recovery capital, heal, and help others to do the same.
http://thesheilasmithfoundation.org/

Voyager Counseling

Olga Montgomery @ Voyager Counseling. I am a radically compassionate women's grief and loss therapist and the founder of Voyager Counseling. I specialize in and am passionate about working with women in their 20's, 30's, & 40's struggling with life-altering loss. I want to help you build your skill and capacity to voyage through your grief experience and orient your life towards your inner true north.
https://www.voyager-counseling.com/

Zeniful

At Zeniful, their mission is to guide clients on a holistic healing journey toward self-discovery, nurturing the harmonious integration of mind, body, and spirit. Allow them to inspire you beyond just DO-ing more to truly BE-ing more, by embodying a life of purposeful presence and authenticity. Are you ready to embrace a life of purpose and presence with us?
https://zeniful.com.au/